Praise for *A Couple Cooks* | *Pretty Simple Cooking*

"So many people are wanting to clean up how they eat, but there is so much information and in so many places, it's overwhelming. Sonja and Alex break it down in this book! I am eager to cook these recipes and also pass this book along to friends and family who need great recipes for the day-to-day meals we seek inspiration for!"

—SARA FORTE, SPROUTEDKITCHEN.COM, AUTHOR OF *SPROUTED KITCHEN*

"I love this cookbook. It's filled with the colorful, delicious brain-healthy foods I prescribe to patients. Cook up some family happiness with them tonight!"

—DREW RAMSEY, MD, NUTRITIONAL PSYCHIATRIST

"Sonja and Alex's recipes spin everyday ingredients into colorful, exciting dishes that are satisfying and healthy. *Pretty Simple Cooking* is the type of book that I could open up on any day and find something delicious to make that I know is going to be special. These pages are going to be soup-stained in no time!"

—MOLLY YEH, MYNAMEISYEH.COM, AUTHOR OF *MOLLY ON THE RANGE*

"Fresh produce shines in *Pretty Simple Cooking*, which offers a delectable range of beautiful and approachable vegetarian recipes. Sonja and Alex offer helpful guidance in the recipes and thoughtful lessons throughout. Whether you're looking for quick, healthy recipes or fresh inspiration, this book is for you. I can't wait to start cooking!"

—KATHRYNE TAYLOR, COOKIEANDKATE.COM, AUTHOR OF *LOVE REAL FOOD*

a couple cooks

PRETTY SIMPLE COOKING

100 Delicious Vegetarian Recipes to
Make You Fall in Love with Real Food

Sonja & Alex Overhiser

Da Capo
LIFE
LONG

Da Capo Press
Hachette Book Group
1290 Avenue of the Americas, New York, NY 10104
www.dacapopress.com
@DaCapoPress

Printed in Canada

First Edition: February 2018

Published by Da Capo Press, an imprint of Perseus Books, LLC, a subsidiary of Hachette Book Group, Inc. The Da Capo Press name and logo is a trademark of the Hachette Book Group.

The publisher is not responsible for websites (or their content) that are not owned by the publisher.

Print book interior design by Tara Long
Illustrations by Ashley Rodriguez

Library of Congress Control Number: 2017953711

ISBNs: 978-0-7382-1969-1 (hardcover), 978-0-7382-1970-7 (ebook)
FRI
10 9 8 7 6 5 4 3 2 1

To Larson Ames,
the dream that came true during the writing of this book

To our family, friends, and readers:
for encouraging an ordinary couple to learn to cook

Contents

Introduction:
Pretty Simple Cooking

"Learn how to cook—try new recipes, learn from your mistakes, be fearless, and above all have fun." JULIA CHILD, *MY LIFE IN FRANCE*

Are You Ready?

Ten years ago, my husband Alex and I set out on a journey. We wanted to know how to cook—and to find food that tasted good and was also good for our bodies. And we knew *nothing*, not one thing about what it took to get there. Fast-forward ten years and we know a thing or two. But what's more important than knowing how to roast a sweet potato or chiffonade basil are the lessons we've learned along the way. The most important one:

YOU HAVE TO FALL IN LOVE.

Cooking is not a one-time transaction, where ingredients go in and food comes out. Cooking requires surrender. It demands expanding your mind to new habits and possibilities. Living in the face of failure. Thinking on your feet, being resourceful.

And the only way to make the kitchen part of your life in the face of these challenges is, really, to fall in love. You must fall in love with the process, the tastes and smells: the fragrance of sizzling garlic, a nutty cinnamon wafting from the oven, the tang of fresh lemon. You must fall in love with making something from nothing.

But challenges abound. Cooking takes time and energy, especially after a long day. The only way you'll keep going is if you start to fall in love with the process. And at the same time, you must also do something else:

YOU HAVE TO CHANGE YOUR MIND.

About food, that is. You have to believe food is worth the time and energy spent preparing it. Worth the money to purchase wholesome ingredients, worth messy kitchens and hungry moments.

Because it *is* worth it. Food has the power to transform your body, your mind, your relationships, and the world around you. Cooking can be one of the most life-giving, fulfilling parts of your day.

We've heard it many times: nourishing, seasonal home cooking is inaccessible, expensive, and impractical for the modern man and woman. We're here to say that with the right attitude, cooking healthy food at home truly can be pretty simple. And so worth it.

Our Story

Speaking of falling in love, that's what happened to Alex and me. We met as awkward, wide-eyed freshmen on the first day of university. I was a young music student from Minnesota, he was an art student from Indiana. They say that love at first sight is real, and though we couldn't articulate it, we found it that day. When he finally asked me on a date, I said no. But he was very, very persistent. And I knew in my gut that I would eventually say yes.

I did, and the rest is history. We got married a few years later and bought a little 1920s bungalow in Indianapolis, with a white picket fence and a tiny galley kitchen. (And a dog, naturally.) After settling in, we decided the next step in life was to invite guests for dinner. The problem was, we didn't know how to make dinner. Our normal rotation of cheesy microwave meals, breakfast cereal, and fast-food tacos certainly wasn't going to cut it.

My first boss lent me a cookbook, written by a woman named Julia Child. The name was meaningless to me, since this was just before Meryl Streep would portray her on-screen in *Julie and Julia*. But as I paged through the book, Julia's personality burst into life. Here was a woman passionate about the act of home cooking, who assured me I could make an omelet with the ease of a Frenchman. Alex's confidence to try new things and zest for learning made him my perfect teammate, and after hours of planning and preparation, we concocted a fancy French dinner of lamb and mashed celery root for our unsuspecting guests. It turned out, well, delicious. We were hooked.

One meal turned to dozens, and soon we were cooking almost daily. Inspired by Mark Bittman's book *Food Matters* and Michael Pollan's mantra, "Eat food. Not too much. Mostly plants," we became inspired by the idea that eating more vegetables could have a positive effect on both personal health and environmental sustainability. We began eating one from-scratch vegetarian meal per week, and a new rainbow of flavors gradually came into focus, like seeing in a new dimension. Our local farmers' market became a playground for fresh food sold to us by the kindest people we'd ever met. The year's rhythm of tomatoes and peaches and kale and squash became our muse. We felt better, had more energy and fewer stomachaches. We got sick less. And most importantly, we felt happier and more fulfilled.

How was it that we spent so much of our lives not knowing food could taste like this? And that I, the girl who couldn't so much as boil a pot of water for pasta, could actually learn to cook? And that it could actually be fun instead of feeling like a chore?

After living twenty-five years in a society obsessed with doing anything but cooking, we were finally learning to feed ourselves. It was 2010, so naturally, we decided to start a blog to document the process. We called it *A Couple Cooks*.

What Is Pretty Simple Cooking?

Our approach to home cooking is pretty simple. Pretty simple cooking:

- Balances beautiful, creative recipes with accessible concepts

- Uses methods that are approachable, though not always quick

- Produces bold, inspired flavors without too many hard-to-find or expensive ingredients

- Features wholesome, seasonal, and quality ingredients

- Emphasizes creativity and playfulness over list making

- Is a lifestyle approach to everyday cooking (page 8)

Here's our not-so-hidden agenda: to inspire your cooking. This book is not here to convert you into any particular diet or way of life. Whether you're a seasoned cook or just starting out, our hope is that you'll find love in the cooking process and that it brings infinite value to your life.

EMBRACING VEG

This book is for eaters of all kinds who want to eat more vegetables and enjoy it. We embrace omnivores, vegetarians, pescatarians, vegans, flexitarians, Paleo eaters, gluten-free eaters, and everything in between. Using trial and error, we encourage you to find the diet that is right for your body and personal tastes.

Alex and I didn't set out to become vegetarian, we just wanted to eat more vegetables—both to improve our health and ease our footprint on the planet. Starting with one meatless meal per week, we gradually increased our veggie-centric eating as we found it to be delicious and enjoyable. We now eat about 80 percent vegetarian on a regular basis; sustainably raised seafood and meat are part of our 20 percent.

Though we're not strictly vegetarian, 100 percent of the recipes in this book are. Why? One of the biggest challenges we hear from people is how to incorporate more vegetables into their diet in a healthy and delicious way. Everyone knows that vegetables are good for us, but many of us carry some boring, bitter, icky vegetable baggage. Whether you eat meatless once a week or every day, we hope you can find recipes you love.

RETHINKING HEALTHY

Healthy used to be a dirty word. Before we started this cooking thing, healthy felt negative, like tasteless low-fat yogurt, cardboard energy bars, and limp salad greens. Healthy was not on our radar. But after ten years of learning and cooking and reading and tasting, we've found that healthy can be flipped to the positive. Our definition of healthy is getting in the kitchen and making meals from scratch—nourishing dishes, heavy on the vegetables, that emphasize flavor rather than the number of calories. Cooking with real food: unprocessed whole ingredients like vegetables and whole grains. Often, this means embracing the seasons and hunting out local ingredients at the farmers' market. And of course, our healthy has plenty of room for guilt-free splurges on the occasional sweet treat.

Since we started eating this way, more and more research has been published on the health benefits of eating whole foods and lots of vegetables. Hospitals and clinics are now starting to prescribe fresh food to prevent and combat disease. An eighty-one-year-old reader wrote to us that our recipes are helping her get her energy back after being diagnosed as diabetic. With more evidence about the benefits of eating fresh food, it's something we believe can be life changing.

EATING FROM THE HEART

To us, eating healthy is more about eating the rainbow of wholesome ingredients and less about rules. It's enjoying gorgeous seasonal produce from our neighborhood farmers' market and learning the names of our local farmers. Buying organic when we can, local when we can. Visiting an organic dairy farm and tasting an artisan aged cheddar. Growing cucumbers in our front lawn, since it's the only place that has sun. Above all, experiencing the tastes of real foods was our most compelling road to healthy. Instead of worrying about ever-changing "rules" or obsessing over calories and omega-3's, we focus on cooking with known healthy ingredients: like loads of leafy greens, sweet potatoes, and whole grains. We lead with intuition, which leaves room for our hearts to crave the good: foods that are good for us, grown in a way that's good for the planet.

> "Our fast food culture has told us that cooking is drudgery. If we had skills before, we've completely lost them. I think we need to go back to school and learn how important it is to feed ourselves with intention."
>
> **ALICE WATERS, *RADIO CHERRY BOMBE*, OCTOBER 15, 2015**

The Secret to Making It Work

This cookbook is a collection of recipes, yes, but it's also about the good stuff: those life lessons that are the difference between a fearless home cook and a person who makes recipes. In the past fifty years, our culture has placed convenience and low cost as the highest priorities for food, persistent ideals that are hard to shake. Thoughtful home cooking with humble ingredients and intentionality doesn't have the seductive marketing of toaster strudels and TV dinners.

We wish we could say that becoming a stellar home cook is as easy as one, two, three, or that there's a magic secret to it all. Unfortunately, there's not. We don't promise our recipes will make you thinner or more beautiful or even happier. But here's what we know: when Alex and I look back on our experience in the home kitchen, we see a handful of guiding principles that turned us from tentative, naïve recipe makers into confident cooks.

The 10 Lessons

There's no quick fix to a sustainable habit of healthy home cooking. Buying a cookbook and blindly following recipes isn't going to cut it, and approaching "healthy" in sprints of 30-day diets may not lead to a long-term habit. But after years of pursuing the art of home cooking, Alex and I have discovered that creativity, intention, and an emotionally healthy approach to food are just as important as nutrition facts and kitchen tools.

There's so much more to food than just what to eat. Through practice, tears, and a whole lot of dirty dishes, we've learned that abiding by these simple lessons makes a joy-filled, pretty simple approach to food possible:

1. Cook real food. (page 11)

2. Slow down. (page 39)

3. Love the (creative) process. (page 73)

4. Face your fear. (page 93)

5. Seek balance. (page 117)

6. Be mindful. (page 129)

7. Yes, you can. (page 145)

8. Gather and share. (page 169)

9. Respect the ingredients. (page 203)

10. Have fun. (page 233)

Our Recipes

Recipes are like clothes. By that, I mean recipes have different functions. When we first started cooking, I figured that a handful of quick and easy main dishes would be all I needed. But imagine having only T-shirts and jeans in your wardrobe. (Okay, some of us may, but hear me out.) What about clothes for work? A rain jacket? A black party dress?

Recipes have different functions, too. Sometimes you're in need of a quick dinner, while other times you have space to make bread or throw a weekend dinner party. This book offers an entire wardrobe of recipes. We've tried to arrange the recipes so you can find the right recipe at the right time. **In this book, recipes at the beginning of each chapter are quickest and simplest, and gradually get more complex and time consuming as you page through the chapter.**

Some recipes are a project—like homemade bread (page 124) or ice cream (page 256)—and that's what makes them fun. Others are a more time-consuming main course for a weekend dinner party. Make these recipes when time allows, like for a family activity or a date night. Remember: simple is not always quick, and planning ahead can make all the difference.

You'll notice that our recipes include simple prep steps for when to slice and dice the ingredients; a little *mise-en-place* goes a long way. Although all the recipes in this book are vegetarian, we've included tips for adding meat where appropriate. Many recipes happen to be gluten-free and vegan and are marked accordingly. Above all, all recipes in this book are designed to fill your heart as well as your stomach.

Four Important Things

Alex and I are often asked for our best kitchen tips. There are a few things we now take for granted that were new to us as beginner cooks:

Use kosher salt. We use kosher salt in our everyday cooking. Avoid substituting table salt for kosher salt. Why? Since the salt granules are flatter, kosher salt is a gentler way to salt food. Whereas table salt can quickly make food taste too salty, kosher salt more easily coaxes out a recipe's natural flavor. Sea salt is a good alternative, but we typically use it as a finishing salt since it can vary widely in size and taste. If you haven't already, buy a big container of kosher salt and keep it in a salt cellar next to your stove.

Taste your food. We learned this from Julia Child. On nearly every one of her cooking shows, she makes the recipe, tastes it, and invariably says it needs "a bit more salt." Before we serve food to anyone, including ourselves, we taste and customize the salt to our liking.

A good knife is worth 1,000 bad ones. Your number one tool is a large, very sharp kitchen knife. We can't emphasize this enough. Thoughtfully choose a knife that works for your hand, and get it sharpened regularly by a professional. When we started cooking, we chose to invest in one good kitchen knife for each of us: while it was an investment at the time, it's lasted us ten years and likely will last ten more.

Recipes are ideas. A recipe is like a chart for a jazz musician: it's an idea, codified to pass it down from one person to the next. All recipes in this book are ideas. As you become a confident cook, feel free to mix and match, substitute one vegetable for another, inspired by the ingredients you have on hand. Take a breakfast recipe and serve it for dinner (and vice versa!). It takes a bit of time to understand what can be modified and what can't, so we've added notes where applicable. Above all, take care to preserve the integrity of the flavor when making changes—like keeping fresh garlic, real lemon juice, and fresh herbs instead of opting for shortcuts.

> ## Creativity, intention, and an emotionally healthy approach to food are just as important as nutrition facts and kitchen tools.

Above All, Have Fun

The main reason Alex and I have kept at seasonal, whole foods home cooking for so long is not because it's good for us (though it is) or because it's good for our relationships and good for the planet (though it is). Those are certainly factors, and they're the reasons that got us started in the kitchen. But the main reason we're still cooking this way is because, well, it's *fun*. It's creative. We love jumping into new experiences together. While we detest list making and planning ahead, we adore the taste of hand-rolled ricotta gnocchi with vodka sauce (page 208). We'd rather make pizza dough with our eight-year-old niece (page 224) instead of ordering in and spending an extra hour on the couch. Our approach is to start before you have it all figured out, otherwise you'll never start. It's not about one-size-fits-all meal plans. It's about falling in love, *literally* falling in love, with the magic of making real, nourishing meals from scratch.

Ready to get started?

"If it came from a plant, eat it;
   if it was made in a plant, don't."

—MICHAEL POLLAN, *FOOD RULES*

Cook real food.

Our world screams opinions on what to eat. Eat this! Fear that! The problem is, scientific understanding of the best way to eat is limited, if there even is a "best" way at all. But there are two simple things most everyone can agree upon. First, real foods made by nature are preferred over engineered foods created by humans. And second, loading up on vegetables is rarely unwise.

Instead of overthinking it, choosing what to eat can be simple: cook whole foods at home and find love in the process. Surround yourself with the best quality ingredients you can access and load up on vegetables. Enjoy seasonal pleasures like juicy peaches in the summer and hearty squash in the autumn. Where possible, support small farmers and producers. Grow a green thumb by nurturing fresh herbs in pots, and then sprinkle them over a morning scramble or a giant salad.

Eating well can be less about reading nutrition labels and counting calories and more about cooking up good, wholesome food.

Breakfast & Brunch

10 MINUTES

California Toast with Roasted Almond Butter and Berries

Soft Scrambled Eggs with Goat Cheese

30-Second Herb and Cheddar Omelet

Toasted Oatmeal

Cherry Almond Breakfast Cereal (Muesli)

Balsamic Blueberry Breakfast Parfait

Strawberry Lime Chia Jam

Cornbread Pancakes with Strawberry Jam

Whole Wheat Weekend Waffles

Huevos Rancheros

Spinach Artichoke Frittata

30 MINUTES

Two-Potato Hash with Romesco

California Toast

with Roasted Almond Butter & Berries

GF* | V | *Serves 4*

California toast is our invention for a special morning meal; it has all the class of French toast but is loads easier. Instead of whisking, soaking, and frying, simply smear toast triangles with almond butter, drizzle with maple syrup, and eat it with a knife and fork. It sounds unassuming, but with crusty multigrain bread, homemade roasted almond butter, juicy berries, and a dusting of cinnamon, it's unexpectedly complex. Make the almond butter in advance or use purchased almond butter for quick assembly—and top with any seasonal fruit or nuts you have on hand.

FOR THE ALMOND BUTTER*

- 2 cups raw almonds
- ½ teaspoon kosher salt
- 1½ tablespoons grapeseed or canola oil

FOR THE TOAST

- 8 slices hearty whole grain bread (purchased or page 124)
- 2 bananas (optional)
- 1 pint fresh seasonal berries of any type
- ½ cup pure maple syrup
- Cinnamon, for garnish

Make the almond butter: Preheat the oven to 325°F.

Spread the almonds on a rimmed baking sheet, then toast for 20 minutes, until fragrant. Let the almonds cool for 1 minute, then transfer to the bowl of the food processor.

Process for 1 minute until dry and crumbly, then stop and scrape down the sides of the bowl. Turn on the processor, then with the motor running add the kosher salt and oil. Continue processing for 5 to 8 minutes, stopping and scraping down the bowl often in the beginning stage and adding a bit more oil if the almonds are too dry. Continue to process until the almonds clump into a large dough ball, and then even longer until the consistency becomes very creamy.

Pour the almond butter into a sealable container or canning jar and store refrigerated for up to 4 weeks (makes 1 cup).

Assemble the toasts: Toast the bread slices. Slice the bananas, if using.

To serve, slather each bread slice with almond butter. Slice the bread into triangles and arrange on a plate, then top with the berries, sliced bananas, and maple syrup. Sprinkle with cinnamon and serve.

Notes
*Substitute ½ cup purchased almond butter.

Use any seasonal fruit: berries in the summer, stone fruit in the late summer, and bananas in the winter. Other topping ideas include balsamic berry compote (page 25), chia jam (page 26), chopped nuts, and pepitas.

GF* For gluten-free, use gluten-free bread.

Scrambled eggs too often turn out hard and rubbery, but this recipe makes soft layers of egg dotted with pillowy clouds of goat cheese. It's my mother's method of gently scraping the eggs into folds over constant medium heat. Here, they're heightened with a bit of tangy goat cheese and the green bite of chives, and it's remarkable how much flavor can be coaxed out of just a few ingredients. We've found that purchasing farmers' market eggs from a vendor who knows our names is absolutely worth the extra dollar—and that eggs from happy chickens taste better too. We make this recipe often using fresh herbs from our garden and whatever cheese we happen to have on hand.

Soft Scrambled Eggs
with Goat Cheese

GF | *Serves 4*

Thinly slice the chives and reserve them as a garnish.

In a medium bowl, whisk the eggs with kosher salt and several grinds of black pepper until well beaten. Break the goat cheese into large crumbles and lightly stir it into the eggs.

In a skillet, melt the butter over medium heat. Tilt the pan to coat the entire surface in melted butter, then pour in the eggs. Continue to cook over medium heat. When the eggs begin to set, about 45 seconds, use a flat spatula to gently scrape sections of eggs, creating folds. Scrape occasionally until the eggs form soft folds, about 1 to 2 minutes, then remove from the heat just before fully hardened.

Garnish with chopped chives and serve immediately.

Notes
Stir in other types of cheese (shredded sharp Cheddar or smoked Gouda) or chopped herbs (thyme, oregano, dill).

1 handful chives, for garnish
8 large eggs
½ teaspoon kosher salt
   Freshly ground black pepper
4 ounces soft goat cheese
2 tablespoons unsalted butter

In her black-and-white TV kitchen, Julia Child urged us to "have the courage of our convictions" and do things we never thought possible, like cook an omelet in a matter of seconds. Her method requires a bit of finesse and bravery, but the more you make it, the better it looks—and tastes. We make omelets individually to order; while they take a few minutes to prep, the cook time is just 30 seconds. This recipe is our simplest classic omelet, which pairs a strong aged Cheddar with chopped garden herbs. Use the recipe as a base and customize the fillings for a special breakfast or a dinner party, using sautéed kale, mushrooms, and peppers, chopped ham and Swiss cheese, or smoked salmon and dill. If it's your first time making an omelet, read the instructions closely before diving in; after a few tries, the technique will become second nature.

30-Second
Herb & Cheddar Omelet

GF | *Serves* **1**

- 1 tablespoon chopped fresh herbs (chives, basil, rosemary, oregano, thyme)
- 2 tablespoons grated sharp Cheddar cheese*
- 2 large eggs
- ⅛ teaspoon kosher salt
  Freshly ground black pepper
- ½ tablespoon unsalted butter

Chop the herbs. Grate the cheese.

In a small bowl, whisk together the eggs, ½ teaspoon water, salt, and several grinds of black pepper until fully combined, about 20 seconds.

Heat a small 8-inch nonstick skillet over just below high heat, with the pan handle facing toward you. Add the butter and swirl the pan to fully coat. Wait until the butter starts to become foamy with large bubbles but not yet browned, then pour in the eggs. When a skin just starts to form (10 to 15 seconds), add the cheese and herbs in a line from left to right across the middle.

Working quickly, run a small spatula under the far edge of the omelet to release it from the pan. Start to pull the eggs up and shake and tilt the pan to spread out any uncooked egg and allow it to cook. Using the spatula, roll the eggs up and over the cheese; this part will be intentionally messy. Cook another 10 to 15 seconds until just barely set; the outside should be a pale golden and the inside soft and creamy (for a harder cooked omelet, cook several seconds longer). Turn off the heat.

To remove the omelet, hold a plate in one hand. Pick up the skillet handle with your right hand, thumb up, and quickly turn the pan upside down over the plate so that the omelet rolls off onto the middle of the plate, folding over itself into a rolled shape. Serve immediately.

Notes
*Our favorite variation: for an elevated omelet, use black truffle Cheddar cheese.

This is not your mama's oatmeal. It's an adaptation from our dear friend Megan Gordon's book *Whole-Grain Mornings*—and once we tried her toasted method, our oatmeal game has never been the same. Toasting the oats on the stovetop before cooking brings out a nutty essence and fills the kitchen with an intoxicating aroma. They're cooked gently so that instead of disintegrating into a gummy slop, each grain retains its shape. Drizzled with a bit of maple syrup, the result is downright divine.

Toasted Oatmeal

GF* | **V*** | *Serves* **2 TO 3**

2 tablespoons unsalted butter

2 cups rolled oats

1 cup 2% milk, plus more for serving (optional)

¼ teaspoon kosher salt

¼ teaspoon cinnamon

¼ cup pecan pieces

Maple syrup, for serving

In a medium saucepan, melt the butter over medium heat. Add the rolled oats and toast until slightly browned and fragrant, stirring constantly, 3 to 4 minutes.

Turn down the heat and immediately add the milk, 1 cup water (omit if using almond milk), kosher salt, and cinnamon. Cook over low heat for 1 minute. Then turn off the heat, cover with a lid, and let stand for 7 minutes. The resulting oats are chewy, not creamy, and may have a bit of milk remaining in the pot.

Meanwhile, in a small skillet over medium-low heat, toast the pecans until fragrant, stirring constantly, 3 to 5 minutes.

To serve, spoon the oatmeal into bowls and top with maple syrup, toasted pecans, and additional milk if desired.

Notes

Storage: Leftovers can be kept refrigerated in a sealed container for up to 5 days.

Other topping ideas include fruit compote (page 25), chia jam (page 26), chopped nuts, and pepitas.

GF* For gluten-free, use gluten-free oats.

V* For vegan, substitute coconut oil for the butter and 2 cups almond milk for the milk (omit the water).

Cherry Almond Breakfast Cereal

(Muesli)

Breakfast cereal was fundamental to both Alex and my mornings growing up; I ate so much I earned the moniker "cereal monster." We later gave up the stuff while transitioning to eating less processed foods, but we've since found a homemade alternative: muesli. In contrast to granola, which can be drowned in oils and sweeteners, muesli is a simple mixture of raw oats, nuts, seeds, and fruit. It's popular in Europe and just starting to come into its own in the United States. For our muesli, we lightly toast the oats and coconut to enhance the texture, then add just a touch of maple syrup and a hint of cozy spices. Dried tart cherries bring it all together. Serve it with milk and a tiny drizzle of maple syrup.

GF* | **V*** | *Makes* **ABOUT 8 CUPS**

- 4 **cups rolled oats**
- 1 **cup unsweetened large coconut flakes (not shredded coconut)**
- 1 **cup whole almonds, roasted and salted**
- 1 **cup dried tart cherries**
- 2 **tablespoons pure maple syrup, plus more for serving**
- 2 **teaspoons vanilla extract**
- ½ **cup pepitas (pumpkin seeds), roasted and salted**
- 1 **teaspoon cinnamon**
- 1 **teaspoon dried ground ginger**
- ½ **teaspoon allspice**
  Milk, for serving

Preheat the oven to 350°F.

Spread out the oats evenly on a baking sheet, then place the coconut in an even layer over the top. Bake 7 to 11 minutes, watching closely, until the coconut is evenly golden brown. Remove from the oven and allow to cool slightly.

Meanwhile, roughly chop the almonds and cherries.

In a small bowl, combine the maple syrup and vanilla, then heat it in the microwave until warmed through and the consistency is thinner, about 20 seconds (alternatively, heat on the stovetop).

In a large bowl, combine the toasted oats and coconut with the cherries, almonds, pepitas, cinnamon, ginger, allspice, and the maple-vanilla mixture, and stir to thoroughly combine. Pour the mixture back onto the baking sheet and spread it into an even layer to allow the muesli to fully dry, about 10 minutes. Stir to break up any clumps, then transfer to a sealable container.

Serve with milk and a touch of maple syrup.

Notes

Storage: Stores indefinitely in the freezer in a sealable bag with the air squeezed out. Serve straight from the freezer—the muesli defrosts almost immediately.

Customize your muesli with other dried fruits, nuts, and seeds to your liking.

GF* For gluten-free, use gluten-free oats.

V* For vegan, serve with coconut or almond milk.

One of the first tricks we learned from Italian cuisine was that the tang of balsamic vinegar enhances the natural sweetness of berries. Here, we've created a rich purple compote by sautéing blueberries and a splash of balsamic, a method that can be used with any berry. Swirled into creamy yogurt, it's a delightful way to breakfast. If you can find it, we recommend grass-fed yogurt for its unique earthiness. The parfaits save well, so refrigerating a few in jars will provide you with breakfasts or snacks throughout the week. They could even stand in for a light summer dessert, topped with chocolate shavings.

Balsamic Blueberry Breakfast Parfait

GF | *Serves 4*

2 cups (1 pint) fresh blueberries

5 tablespoons pure maple syrup, divided

2 teaspoons balsamic vinegar

3 cups plain Greek or grass-fed yogurt

½ cup chopped pecans

Cinnamon, for garnish

Wash the blueberries. In a large skillet, heat the blueberries, 2 tablespoons maple syrup, and the balsamic vinegar over medium heat until the blueberries just start to break down and form a purple syrup, 4 to 8 minutes. Remove from the heat and allow to cool to room temperature, 5 to 10 minutes.

Meanwhile, stir together the yogurt and 3 tablespoons maple syrup.

In four 2-cup mason jars or glasses, layer ½ cup yogurt, a large spoonful of berries with syrup, and 1 tablespoon chopped pecans, then another ¼ cup of yogurt, more berries, and more pecans. Top with a sprinkle of cinnamon.

Notes

Storage: Cover with a lid and refrigerate for 2 to 3 days.

Use other seasonal berries in place of the blueberries (raspberries, blackberries, or sliced strawberries), and other nuts in place of the pecans (walnuts, pistachios, or almonds).

Tip: Vegan "dairy" products are starting to come into their own and several brands offer high-quality flavor and texture. Feel free to experiment with vegan yogurts for this recipe and vegan dairy products as substitutions in other recipes in the book.

Strawberry Lime Chia Jam

Chia jam is a revelation. When heated, the tiny seeds naturally thicken fruit into a jelly-like spread, making for supremely simple homemade preserves. This jam features strawberries, maple syrup, and lime for a tangy punch. Spread it on toast, swirl it in yogurt, or use it for topping pancakes (page 29). The omega-3's in chia seeds and the natural sweetener make it a nourishing version of traditional jam—but the flavor is what will have you hooked.

GF | V | *Makes* 2 CUPS

2 cups frozen strawberries*

2 tablespoons lime juice plus zest (1 large lime)

6 tablespoons pure maple syrup

1 teaspoon vanilla extract

3 tablespoons chia seeds

In a 10-inch skillet, add the strawberries, lime juice, and 2 tablespoons water. Simmer over medium heat for 10 minutes, stirring occasionally. About halfway through the simmering time, begin to break down the berries by smashing them with a fork into a chunky but uniform texture.

Once the berries are broken down, stir in the maple syrup, vanilla, chia seeds, and lime zest until combined, about 30 seconds. Turn off the heat. Let the skillet sit about 5 to 7 minutes until the chia seeds thicken the jam. Transfer to a 16-ounce canning jar and refrigerate; the texture will set even further when chilled.

Notes

Storage: Stores refrigerated for up to 2 weeks (chia jam is not shelf stable).

*One pound of fresh strawberries can be substituted for frozen, which cuts the simmering time to around half. However, we prefer using frozen berries for jams and saving fresh ones for eating.

Instead of a plateful of refined white flour and sugar, these cornbread pancakes are made mostly of masa harina: a fine corn flour that's traditionally used to make tortillas. This flour keeps them fluffy and adds a complexity that takes them a notch above the standard pancake. Topped with a smear of strawberry chia jam, it's a lightly sweet, special-occasion breakfast. If desired, add some nut butter for PB&J, a handful of chopped nuts, or a drizzle of crème fraîche. We also love these flapjacks savory, topped with sour cream and chopped chives.

Cornbread Pancakes

with Strawberry Jam

GF* | *Makes **8 TO 10 PANCAKES***

- 1 **cup masa harina***
- ½ **cup all-purpose, whole wheat, or gluten-free flour**
- 1 **teaspoon baking soda**
- ½ **teaspoon kosher salt**
- 2 **large eggs**
- 3 **tablespoons neutral oil (grapeseed or vegetable)**
- 2 **tablespoons honey or pure maple syrup**
- ½ **cup plain Greek yogurt**
- 1 **cup 2% milk**
- **Maple syrup, for serving (optional)**
- **Strawberry Lime Chia Jam (page 26), for serving (optional)**
- **Roasted almond butter (page 14), for serving (optional)**
- **Crème fraîche (page 139), for serving (optional)**

Preheat the oven to 200°F.

In a medium bowl, stir together the masa harina, flour, baking soda, and kosher salt. In another bowl, whisk together the eggs, oil, honey or maple syrup, Greek yogurt, and milk. Pour the dry ingredients into the wet ingredients, then stir gently to combine until the batter comes together and is pourable but slightly lumpy.

Heat a large nonstick griddle or skillet over medium-low heat, then brush with butter or oil. Scoop a scant ⅓ cup of batter onto the griddle and repeat to make 4 pancakes. Cook for several minutes until a few of the bubbles that appear on the surface have burst and the bottoms are golden brown, adjusting the heat as necessary. Flip carefully, then cook for another minute or so until golden brown on the other side.

Place the cooked pancakes on a baking sheet in the oven to keep warm. Add a splash of milk to the remaining batter to loosen it. Then repeat for the remaining pancakes, adjusting the heat as necessary since the griddle can become very hot. Serve warm with maple syrup, roasted almond butter, Strawberry Lime Chia Jam, or crème fraîche.

Notes

Storage: To store leftovers, allow the pancakes to fully cool. Place them in a sealed container in the refrigerator for 3 to 5 days. Reheat in a toaster, in a 200°F oven, or on a griddle until warm.

*Masa harina can be found in the international foods aisle in most grocery stores, or online. Do not substitute cornmeal.

GF* For gluten-free, use gluten-free flour.

Whole Wheat Weekend Waffles

These fluffy waffles are just the thing for slanted Saturday morning light and a warm cup of coffee. They're dairy-free, made with coconut oil and almond milk and a touch of whole wheat flour. But most importantly, they're crispy and light, a fitting canvas for topping art. Get as creative as you'd like with the toppings: we like a sprinkle of chopped nuts, a dollop of honey-sweetened Greek yogurt, and good old maple syrup.

GF* | *Serves 4*

- 1 cup all-purpose flour
- ½ cup whole wheat flour
- 2 teaspoons baking powder
- ½ teaspoon cinnamon
- ¼ teaspoon allspice
- ½ teaspoon kosher salt
- 1 large egg
- ¼ cup coconut oil, melted and slightly cooled
- 1¼ cups unsweetened almond milk
- 1 teaspoon vanilla extract
- 2 tablespoons pure maple syrup

Preheat a waffle iron to the high heat setting.

In a medium bowl, mix the all-purpose flour, whole wheat flour, baking powder, cinnamon, allspice, and kosher salt until thoroughly combined.

In another bowl, whisk the egg. Then stir in the melted coconut oil, almond milk, vanilla extract, and maple syrup. Pour the wet ingredients into the dry ingredients and mix gently until just combined; do not overmix.

Immediately, add a generous ½ cup batter into the center of the waffle iron and let it spread it to within ½ inch of the sides; cook according to the waffle iron's instructions. Remove the cooked waffles and place them on a baking sheet without stacking. Make the waffles to order, or place cooked waffles in a 300°F oven to keep warm. Serve with your desired toppings.

Notes

Storage: Cooked waffles can be frozen in an airtight plastic bag. To reheat, remove from the freezer and lightly toast in a toaster.

Topping ideas: maple syrup, fresh fruit (berries, peaches, plums, bananas, mango), balsamic blueberry compote (page 25), Strawberry Lime Chia Jam (page 26), roasted almond butter (page 14), or coconut whipped cream (page 236), Greek yogurt with a touch of honey, chopped nuts (walnuts, almonds, pistachios), or fruit jams or preserves.

GF* For gluten-free, use gluten-free flour.

Think two Midwesterners can't make huevos? Our light, fresh take on the traditionally heavy huevos rancheros has received the green light from several native Texans we know. Instead of fried, the tortillas are baked until just crispy, then topped with a savory red sauce, gooey egg, and sprinkling of feta cheese. Chipotle powder brings a gentle heat and smokiness to the sauce that can't be replicated otherwise. Serve them with Simple Refried Pinto Beans for a hearty breakfast or brunch. Honestly, we eat them even more often as a simple dinner.

Huevos Rancheros

GF | *Serves 4*

Preheat the oven to 400°F.

If serving with Simple Refried Pinto Beans, start the beans.

Peel and mince the onion. In a medium saucepan, heat the olive oil over medium-high heat. Add the onion and sauté until translucent, 3 to 5 minutes. Add the tomatoes, chili powder, cumin, chipotle powder, and ¼ teaspoon kosher salt. Bring it to a simmer, then cover and allow to simmer, gently bubbling, for about 15 minutes, while preparing the remainder of the recipe.

Meanwhile, brush both sides of each tortilla with olive oil. Place the tortillas on a baking sheet and bake for 2 to 3 minutes on each side until lightly browned and crisp, yet still slightly flexible (the timing varies based on your oven and brand of tortillas). Remove from the oven and set aside until serving.

In a large skillet, melt ½ tablespoon of the butter over medium heat. Add 4 of the eggs and sprinkle with a pinch of kosher salt and several grinds of black pepper. Cook for 2 to 3 minutes, until the whites are firm (do not flip). Remove the eggs from the pan to a plate, then melt another ½ tablespoon butter and fry the remaining 4 eggs.

To serve, slide each egg on top of a crispy tortilla, then top with a dollop of tomato sauce, torn cilantro leaves, and queso fresco. Serve 2 eggs per person, and add a side of refried beans and sliced avocado for a hearty meal.

Simple Refried Pinto Beans (page 102), for serving (optional)

1 small white onion

1 tablespoon extra-virgin olive oil, plus more for brushing

1 15-ounce can crushed tomatoes

½ teaspoon chili powder

1 teaspoon cumin

¼–½ teaspoon chipotle powder or cayenne (depending on your spice tolerance)

¼ teaspoon kosher salt, plus more for the eggs

8 corn tortillas

1 tablespoon unsalted butter

8 large eggs

Freshly ground black pepper

1 handful cilantro, for serving

Queso fresco or feta cheese crumbles, for serving

Sliced avocado, for serving (optional)

Spinach Artichoke Frittata

Frittatas work any time of day: brunch, lunch, or even a simple dinner with a green salad. This is the one we make most often, featuring the classic dip combination, spinach and artichoke. Using sour cream instead of milk in the frittata base makes gooey, creamy pockets. An alternative to the classic baked egg casserole, it's made in almost half the time and baked right in a skillet.

GF | *Serves 4 TO 6*

2 green onions

1 medium garlic clove

1 15-ounce can quartered artichoke hearts

8 large eggs

½ teaspoon dried oregano

½ teaspoon plus pinch kosher salt

Freshly ground black pepper

½ cup sour cream or crème fraîche, plus more for serving

¼ cup shredded Parmesan cheese

1 tablespoon extra-virgin olive oil

6 cups baby spinach leaves, loosely packed (chopped if leaves are large)*

Preheat the oven to 400°F.

Thinly slice the green onions. Mince the garlic. Drain the artichoke hearts and roughly chop them, removing any tough leaves.

In a medium bowl, whisk together the eggs, oregano, kosher salt, and several grinds of black pepper. Whisk in the sour cream and Parmesan cheese until mostly incorporated; small clumps of sour cream can remain.

In a 10-inch oven-safe skillet, heat the olive oil over medium heat. Sauté the spinach, stirring until wilted, 2 to 3 minutes. Add the green onions, garlic, and artichokes, and sauté for another minute, stirring and pulling some of the spinach to the top of the vegetable mixture.

Pour the egg mixture into the skillet; if necessary, shake the skillet gently to allow the eggs to fill in around the vegetables. Cook about 5 to 7 minutes over medium heat until the bottom is set and lightly browned, checking for doneness by pulling back the side with a spatula.

Place the skillet in the oven and bake 10 to 12 minutes until the top is puffed, set, and slightly browned. Let rest for 10 minutes, then cut into wedges and serve warm, with additional sour cream or crème fraîche, if desired.

Notes
*Other greens can stand in for spinach, like chopped kale or chard.

Frittatas are a great place for experimentation once you've mastered the concept. Substitute sautéed chopped vegetables (onion, peppers, kale, chard, zucchini, mushrooms) or cooked meat (sausage or chicken) for the filling.

The secret to this hash is in the romesco, a Spanish sauce made of tomato, almonds, and red pepper, punctuated with tangy sherry vinegar and smoked paprika. I first fell in love with smoked paprika while living in Madrid a few years back, and since then Alex and I have found it adds a smoky depth to vegetarian dishes, like paella (page 194), lentil stew (page 167), or even mayonnaise (page 152). Typically, the red-orange romesco sauce is served with fish or poultry, but here we've used it to amp up potatoes in a breakfast hash. It's a satisfying vegan breakfast for two, or add a fried egg on top to extend the serving size to four.

Two-Potato Hash
with Romesco

GF | V* | *Serves* 2 TO 4*

Make the romesco: Peel the garlic. In the bowl of a food processor or blender, place the garlic, almonds, diced tomatoes and their juices, red pepper, smoked paprika, vinegar, olive oil, and kosher salt. Blend on high until smooth. Taste and adjust seasonings as desired.

Make the hash: Dice the potatoes into ½-inch or smaller cubes, leaving the skin on. In a large skillet (12 inches or larger), heat the olive oil over medium-high heat. Add the potatoes, 1 teaspoon kosher salt, and several grinds of black pepper. Sauté for 15 to 17 minutes, flipping the potatoes often with a spatula, until browned and crisp.

Meanwhile, thinly slice the green onion or chives.

When the potatoes are done, remove them from the skillet into a bowl. Place the skillet back over medium heat and add the spinach, 2 pinches of kosher salt, and several grinds of black pepper, then sauté for 1 to 2 minutes until the spinach is wilted. Add the potatoes back to the pan and mix to combine with the spinach.

Fry the eggs (optional): If desired, add a drizzle of olive oil to the skillet and bring to medium heat. Add the eggs and cook sunny side up until the whites have hardened. Sprinkle with a bit of kosher salt and black pepper.

To serve, garnish the potatoes with sliced green onion or chives, and serve with romesco sauce.

Notes
Storage: Store leftover sauce in a sealed container in the refrigerator for up to 1 week.

***Adding a fried egg can extend the serving size to 4. For a vegan breakfast for 4, double the potatoes and fry them in two batches.

V* For vegan, omit the optional egg.

FOR THE ROMESCO
- 1 small garlic clove
- 1 cup roasted almonds
- 1 15-ounce can diced tomatoes
- 1 large roasted red pepper, from a jar
- 2 teaspoons smoked paprika (pimentón)
- 2 tablespoons sherry vinegar or red wine vinegar
- 1 tablespoon extra-virgin olive oil
- ¼ teaspoon kosher salt

FOR THE HASH
- 1 pound sweet potatoes
- 1 pound russet potatoes
- 3 tablespoons extra-virgin olive oil, plus more for frying
- 1 teaspoon plus 2 pinches kosher salt, divided

  Freshly ground black pepper, divided
- 1 green onion or 1 handful chives, for garnish
- 5 cups baby spinach leaves, loosely packed (chopped if leaves are large)
- 4 large eggs (optional)

"Our kitchens and other eating places more and more resemble filling stations. We hurry through our meals to go to work and hurry through our work in order to 'recreate' ourselves in the evenings and on weekends and vacations."

—WENDELL BERRY,
THE PLEASURES OF EATING

Slow down.

We live in a culture with increasing demands on our time. Bigger, better, faster—there's always more to do and not enough time to do it. Slowing down is painful. In many ways, it's easier to be addicted to the busy.

To make room for eating well, some things may need to be let go—like procrastination, disorganization, or an over-scheduled daily life. But in the process of slowing down, cooking can become less of a chore and more of an outlet for relaxation. You may find solace in the rhythm of the knife blade or the sizzle of the onions as they meet the pan. Even better, those "lost" minutes cooking may be gained back in other ways. Time spent cooking for family and friends is the ultimate in multitasking: it provides nourishment, quality time, and entertainment all in one.

Cooking takes much more than just simple know-how. It requires stepping back, slowing down, making priorities, and developing new life rhythms—rhythms that can be truly satisfying.

Starters & Snacks

Creamy Artichoke Hummus

GF | V | *Makes* **2 CUPS**

Everyone has a household hummus recipe, and here's ours—which takes just 5 minutes and 5 ingredients (plus salt). The artichokes bring an unexpected tang and a supremely creamy texture that doesn't solidify in the refrigerator like many homemade hummus recipes. Tahini is essential to a good hummus; the ground sesame paste keeps for months and can be used for creamy, dairy-free drizzling sauces (like our Burrito Bowl with Cumin Lime Crema on page 187 and Turmeric Rice Bowls with Lemon Tahini Drizzle on page 200).

- 1 small garlic clove
- 1 15-ounce can chickpeas
- 1 15-ounce can artichoke hearts, packed in water
- ¼ cup tahini
- ¾ teaspoon kosher salt
- ½ lemon

Peel the garlic. Drain the chickpeas (no need to rinse). Drain the artichoke hearts into a liquid measuring cup.

To the bowl of a food processor or blender, add the garlic, chickpeas, artichoke hearts, tahini, and kosher salt, and purée for a few seconds until combined. Slowly add the artichoke water a few tablespoons at a time until a creamy texture is reached, stopping to taste and make adjustments as needed. The amount of liquid you add will depend on the texture of the tahini and may be different each time you make it. Continue processing for 1 to 2 minutes until the texture is fluffy. Add a few squeezes of lemon juice, to taste.

Notes

Storage: Store refrigerated for 7 to 10 days.

If desired, serve with a sprinkle of paprika, a drizzle of olive oil, and fresh chopped cilantro.

Of all the recipes we serve to guests, this is one people consistently go mad for. A dear friend first served it to us over wine and conversation in her cozy kitchen. We asked for the recipe, which she adapted from a torn-out page of *Everyday Food* magazine, and we have been serving our version of it ever since. Nearly every time we make it, we're asked for the recipe too! It's fantastic with crackers or crostini and works as a vegetable dip as well. For an extra kick, top it with our quick chili oil.

Irresistible Tomato Almond Dip

GF | V | *Makes* **2 CUPS**

Make the dip: Peel the garlic. Add the almonds and garlic to the bowl of a food processor and pulse until roughly chopped. Add the tomatoes, paprika, balsamic vinegar, kosher salt, red pepper flakes, and olive oil. Process until the nuts are thoroughly combined, about 10 seconds. Scrape down the sides of the bowl and pulse a few more seconds to achieve a thick, creamy texture. Stir in 1 to 2 pinches kosher salt to taste. Serve with crackers or bread.

Make the chili oil (optional): In a small skillet, warm the olive oil with the red pepper flakes over low heat for 3 to 5 minutes. Drizzle the chili oil over the dip before serving.

Notes
Storage: Store refrigerated for up to 7 days.

FOR THE DIP
- 1 small garlic clove
- ¾ cup roasted unsalted almonds
- 1 15-ounce can crushed fire-roasted tomatoes
- 1 tablespoon sweet paprika
- 1 tablespoon balsamic vinegar
- ½ teaspoon kosher salt
- 2 pinches red pepper flakes
- 3 tablespoons extra-virgin olive oil

FOR THE CHILI OIL
- 1 tablespoon extra-virgin olive oil
- 2 pinches red pepper flakes

Garlic Herb White Bean Dip

Made with cannellini beans, this herby dip is an alternative to hummus, and its creamy texture pairs well with crisp vegetables or Baked Pita Crisps (page 61). We make it especially often in the summer months when the clay pots on our front steps are overflowing with fragrant green herbs. We like using a mix of fresh garden herbs, but a single herb can be used for a more straightforward flavor.

GF | **V** | *Makes* **2 CUPS**

- 2 15-ounce cans cannellini beans
- 1 medium garlic clove
- ½ cup packed fresh herbs (basil, thyme, oregano, chives, rosemary*)
- ¼ cup extra-virgin olive oil
- 2 tablespoons white wine vinegar
- ¾ teaspoon kosher salt
  Freshly ground black pepper

Drain and rinse the beans. Peel the garlic. Remove any tough stems from the herbs.

In the bowl of a food processor, add the garlic and the herbs and process until finely chopped. Then add the beans, olive oil, white wine vinegar, ½ teaspoon kosher salt, and several grinds of black pepper to the bowl of the food processor. Process until very smooth, then taste and add the remaining ¼ teaspoon kosher salt if desired. Scrape down the bowl and process again for 30 seconds until light and fluffy.

Notes
Storage: Store refrigerated for up to 7 days.

*If using rosemary, a little goes a long way.

In the winter when herbs are not as abundant, substitute a spoonful of jarred pesto.

Our Top Herbs to Grow

If you don't have a green thumb, growing herbs can be intimidating. They're actually quite simple to grow. Find a few pots, plant the herbs (seeds or starts) about 8 inches apart, set them in the sun, and make sure they're watered daily. Here are the top herbs we grow in our garden. Typically, we buy Italian parsley and cilantro at the store; we've found they don't grow easily at home.

01. Basil	03. Thyme	05. Dill	07. Rosemary
02. Chives	04. Mint	06. Oregano	08. Sage

We've had some top-notch mentors for this homemade salsa. On our podcast, we interviewed Chef Rick Bayless, the renowned restaurateur, author, and TV show host, and he taught us to add charred peppers for a smoky undertone to our salsas. After enjoying the salsa at a Miami taco joint, Taquiza, we consulted with Chef Steve Santana for a few final tweaks to our recipe. His advice: Increase the salt and lime, and strain out excess liquid. The result is a zesty, restaurant-style salsa that makes an ample amount, almost double the typical store-bought jar. Enjoy it with Homemade Tortilla Chips (page 58) or over Loaded Sweet Potato Wedges with Black Beans (page 184).

Roasted Poblano Salsa

GF | V | *Makes* **3 CUPS**

2 poblano peppers
½ large white onion
1 medium garlic clove
½ jalapeño pepper
1 28-ounce can diced tomatoes
1 tablespoon apple cider vinegar
1 tablespoon lime juice (½ lime)
1½ teaspoons kosher salt

Roast the poblanos, onion, and garlic: Cut the tops from the poblano peppers, then cut them in half lengthwise and remove the white membrane and seeds. Peel the onion and slice it into rough chunks. Peel the garlic. Place the peppers, garlic, and onion on the sheet, and broil on high for about 7 minutes until starting to blacken and soften, then flip and roast on the other side for about 5 minutes. Remove from the oven and allow to cool for 1 minute.

Make the salsa: Meanwhile, slice the jalapeño pepper in half, taking care to properly shield your hands and eyes. Remove the ribs and seeds. Reserve the seeds (for a hot salsa) along with half of the pepper.

In the bowl of a food processor, pulse the poblano peppers, onion, garlic, and half of the jalapeño pepper several times until roughly chopped. Add the diced tomatoes, apple cider vinegar, lime juice, and kosher salt, and process until the desired texture is reached. Taste and add seeds or the remaining half jalapeño pepper, according to your spice preference.

Pour the salsa into a sealable container. If time allows, refrigerate for at least 30 minutes, then pour into a strainer, strain out the extra liquid, and return it to the container.

Notes
Storage: Store refrigerated for up to 7 days.

Peach Salsa Fresca

One of the first recipes Alex and I learned to make together early in our marriage was mango salsa, which we served over grilled fish. I was delighted by the sweet and savory play of flavors, and to this day I feel nostalgia for it as one of the recipes that started it all. This version is the same idea with a fruit grown in our Midwest locale: juicy summer peaches. Save this recipe for high summer when the ripest of peaches are available. Serve with Homemade Tortilla Chips (page 58) or alongside grilled fish or shrimp.

GF | V | *Makes* **3 CUPS**

 4 ripe peaches (about 1½ pounds)*
 ¼ cup minced red onion
 1 serrano pepper
 ¼ cup chopped cilantro
 2 tablespoons lime juice (1 large lime)
 ¼ teaspoon kosher salt

Finely dice the peaches. Peel and mince the red onion. Halve the serrano pepper; remove the ribs and reserve the seeds (for a hot salsa). Mince the pepper, reserving half. Chop the cilantro. Juice the lime.

Combine the peaches, onion, half of the minced pepper, cilantro, lime juice, and kosher salt, and stir to combine. Taste and add seeds or the remaining half serrano pepper, according to your spice preference. Serve immediately (do not refrigerate).

Notes
Storage: This salsa is best served immediately the day it is made. It accumulates liquid as it sits, so it may need to be drained if made a few hours in advance.

*Substitute 2 ripe mangoes for the peaches if desired.

Alex's family lives in Indiana farmland, not too far from a beekeeper. A gentle man with a white beard and a kind smile, he invited us for a tour after learning of my infatuation with the sticky natural sweetener. A few golden half-gallon jars later, we left in awe of the intense work ethic of the tiny bees and their intricate social life (queen bees! royal jelly!). Ever since, we buy local honey—both for the nuanced flavor and to support local pollinators. Here, thyme-infused honey is the key to our basic formula for a top-notch crostini, featuring creamy, savory goat cheese and tangy plums. Any seasonal fruit can stand in: peaches, strawberries, or blackberries in the summer, or apple, cranberries, or dried cherries in the winter. The mix of sweet, savory, soft, and crunchy is the ultimate appetizer accompanied by a glass of wine.

Goat Cheese & Thyme Honey Crostini

GF* | **V*** | *Makes* **24 CROSTINI**

- 1 crusty baguette
- 1 teaspoon finely chopped fresh thyme leaves*
- 2 tablespoons honey, plus more for garnish (local, if possible)
- 4 plums or 1 large apple
- 4 ounces soft goat cheese

Preheat the oven to 400°F.

Make the crostini: Slice the baguette on the bias into 24 ½-inch slices. Place the slices in a single layer on a baking sheet and toast 7 to 14 minutes, until slightly browned and crisp.

Make the thyme honey: Finely chop the thyme and set it aside. In a small saucepan, mix the honey with 2 teaspoons of water; heat until warmed through and easy to drizzle (alternatively, heat in the microwave for 10 seconds). Stir in the thyme.

Assemble the crostini: Slice the plums or apple. (If not serving immediately, mix the apple slices with a bit of lemon juice to prevent them from browning.) Spread each crostini with goat cheese, then top with plum or apple slices and a drizzle of thyme honey. Serve immediately.

GF* For gluten-free, use gluten-free bread or crackers.

V* For vegan, use spreadable vegan cheese.

Layered Mediterranean Hummus Platter

This stunning dip is inspired by our time in the sunny Greek isles, featuring briny Kalamata olives, salty feta, and tangy artichoke hearts. It's a wholesome version of a seven-layer dip that looks impressive but is quite simple to put together. You can use purchased hummus and pita chips for easy entertaining, or make our Creamy Artichoke Hummus (page 42) and Baked Pita Crisps (page 61) in advance. Alex and I make this platter as part of a "happy hour dinner" along with a cheese board (page 57) and wine for summer evenings on the patio.

GF* | **V*** | *Serves* **4 TO 6**

¼ cup minced red onion

½ cup chopped cucumber

½ cup (7 ounces) chopped canned artichoke hearts

¼ cup chopped Kalamata olives

½ cup quartered cherry tomatoes or ½ cup diced red bell pepper (fresh or jarred)

1½ cups (12 ounces) hummus or 1 recipe Creamy Artichoke Hummus (page 42)

¼ cup crumbled feta cheese

1 handful cilantro, for garnish

Paprika, for garnish

Squeeze of lemon, for garnish

Pita chips or Baked Pita Crisps (page 61), for serving

Peel and mince the red onion. Rinse the minced onion under cool water and squeeze dry (to remove some of the bite). Peel the cucumber and remove the seeds with a spoon; chop into bite-sized pieces. Chop the artichoke hearts. Roughly chop the olives. Quarter the cherry tomatoes or dice the pepper.

Spread the hummus on a large plate and top with the red onion, cucumber, artichokes, olives, tomatoes, and feta cheese. Sprinkle the hummus with torn cilantro leaves and paprika and top with a squeeze of lemon juice. Serve with pita crisps.

GF* For gluten-free, use gluten-free pita crisps or crackers.

V* For vegan, omit the feta cheese and top with a few pinches of kosher salt.

The perfect cheese board looks simple at a glance, but selecting the right cheeses and accoutrements can be tricky. We recommend finding 4 to 5 different cheeses that fit a loose theme: like 5 different cheddar cheeses or 4 French-made cheeses. For this one, we've gone global and picked contrasting cheeses from different regions: pungent, mild, soft, and hard. When purchasing cheese, note that smaller independent cheese shops or gourmet groceries tend to have more options than the standard supermarket cheese counter, without much of a difference in cost. For the accoutrements, a variety of fruits, nuts, olives, and bread can be so satisfying you hardly feel the need to eat dinner at all.

World-Traveler Cheese Board

GF* | V* | *Serves* 8

About 1 hour before serving, remove the cheese from refrigerator and bring to room temperature. Serve with accoutrements.

GF* For gluten-free, use gluten-free crackers or bread.

V* For vegan, consider a high-quality vegan cheese (ask your grocer for recommendations).

4 ounces American artisanal goat cheese

4 ounces English white Cheddar or French blue cheese

4 ounces Spanish manchego cheese

4 ounces Italian aged Parmesan, Asiago, or Pecorino cheese

Crostini (page 53) or assorted crackers

Spicy mustard

Apricot jam, citrus marmalade, or other locally made preserves

Seedless grapes

Sliced apples

Dried figs

Mixed pickles (see Crunchy Dill and Curry Cauliflower Quick Pickles on page 70)

Olives (see Rosemary Olives with Lemon Zest on page 69)

Salted almonds

Homemade Tortilla Chips

GF | V | *Serves 6*

It's easy to buy a bag of tortilla chips, but there's something rewarding about making your own at home—and it cuts down on the urge to overconsume a big bag of chips. Since we typically have tortillas in the refrigerator, we started to make our chips on demand. Simply brush tortillas with olive oil, slice into wedges, dust with salt, and bake. Quality tortillas are key here: for best results, use thin, authentic-style corn tortillas that are pliable and not overly dry. Serve with Roasted Poblano Salsa (page X) or Peach Salsa Fresca (page X), or top them with rice, beans, salsa, and Creamy Cashew Sauce (page X) for makeshift nachos.

12 corn tortillas
1–2 tablespoons extra-virgin olive oil
    Flaked sea salt

Preheat the oven to 350°F.

Brush the tortillas with olive oil on both sides, then use a pizza cutter to slice them into 8 wedges per tortilla.

Line two baking sheets with parchment paper or silicone mats. Place the wedges in a single layer on the sheets and lightly sprinkle them with salt, crushing the salt with your fingers as you sprinkle. Bake until golden and crispy, 15 to 20 minutes, rotating the pans halfway through. Remove from the oven and allow to cool. Tortilla chips are best fresh from the oven.

Notes
Storage: Store in an airtight container at room temperature up to 1 week.

Packaged chips and crackers were one of the first things to go when we decided to minimize the processed foods in our pantry. A few simple homemade recipes now satisfy our snacking needs, like these pita chips. They're seasoned with salt and garlic and baked until crisp. Making them from scratch enhances the taste—and skips the long list of preservatives in many store-bought brands. Dip them in Creamy Artichoke Hummus (page 42), Garlic Herb White Bean Dip (page 46), or Irresistible Tomato Almond Dip (page 45).

Baked Pita Crisps

GF* | V | *Serves 8*

Preheat the oven to 350°F.

Brush each pita with olive oil on both sides. Sprinkle each side with 1 generous pinch of kosher salt and 1 small pinch of garlic powder (optional). Using a pizza cutter, cut each pita into 8 wedges.

Line two baking sheets with parchment paper or silicone mats. Place the wedges in a single layer on the sheets. Bake until lightly browned and crisp: 13 to 15 minutes for thinner pita bread and 20 to 23 minutes for thicker pita bread, rotating the sheets halfway through the baking time. Allow to cool. Serve as wedges, or break into irregular bite-sized pieces.

Notes

Storage: Store in an airtight container at room temperature up to 1 week.

GF* For gluten-free, use purchased gluten-free pita bread.

4 whole wheat pita breads
2 tablespoons extra-virgin olive oil
   Kosher salt
   Garlic powder (optional)

Baked Goat Cheese

with Tomato Sauce

This baked goat cheese is our take on a dish served at Napolese, our go-to neighborhood pizzeria. To us, the appetizer is just as satisfying as the pizza. Quality canned tomatoes are key here; we recommend finding the best variety and brand possible. Typically, we use San Marzano tomatoes, a variety grown in Italy that's now widely available canned—which we also use for our artisan-style pizza (page 222). We serve this one with slices of crusty bread (page 126) or naan (page 122) for dipping. But we like it best as a light dinner for two with a bottle of red and some marinated olives— so we don't have to share.

GF* | *Serves 4*

½ cup chopped white onion

2 medium garlic cloves

1 tablespoon extra-virgin olive oil, plus more for garnish

1 tablespoon plus 1 teaspoon chopped fresh basil or ¼ teaspoon dried

½ tablespoon red pepper flakes (or less, to taste)

¼ teaspoon dried oregano

½ tablespoon white wine vinegar

1 15-ounce can crushed tomatoes, San Marzano or fire roasted, if possible

½ teaspoon kosher salt

Freshly ground black pepper

4 ounces soft goat cheese

Baguette or crusty bread, for serving

Preheat the oven to 375°F.

Peel and finely mince the onion. Peel and mince the garlic. Chop the basil.

In a saucepan, heat the olive oil over medium heat. Add the onion and sauté for 3 minutes, then add the garlic, red pepper flakes, 1 tablespoon fresh basil (¼ teaspoon dried), and oregano, and sauté for 1 minute. Add the white wine vinegar and stir for 1 minute, then carefully add the tomatoes, kosher salt, and several grinds of black pepper. Reduce the heat, cover, and allow to simmer, lightly bubbling, for 10 minutes. Taste and adjust seasonings as desired.

Spoon the tomato sauce into shallow baking dishes or ramekins, then add dollops of goat cheese. Bake until the cheese is warmed through, about 15 minutes. If desired, broil for a minute or two to brown the top of the cheese. Allow to cool for a few minutes, then top with 1 teaspoon of fresh basil (optional) and a drizzle of olive oil. Serve warm with crusty bread.

Notes

For a larger appetizer, the recipe doubles easily: use a 28-ounce can of tomatoes and double the remainder of the ingredients.

GF* For gluten-free, use gluten-free bread.

These roasted sweet potato rounds are one of our most requested recipes by friends and family, and many times one of the few vegetable-based choices at a party snack table. We've created two variations here: Classic is topped with Mexican hot sauce, and Hot Wings with blue cheese and Frank's RedHot sauce. Both are sprinkled with almond bacon: sliced almonds drenched in a soy and liquid smoke mixture that make a salty topping reminiscent of the real stuff. These bites are great party food, but we've also heard of people eating them as a meal (for example, us!).

Famous Loaded Sweet Potato Rounds

GF* | **V*** | *Serves* **4 TO 6**

FOR THE SWEET POTATOES

- 2 pounds sweet potatoes (small, thin potatoes are best)
- 2 tablespoons extra-virgin olive oil
- 1 teaspoon garlic powder
- 1 teaspoon chili powder
- 1 teaspoon kosher salt

FOR THE ALMOND BACON (OPTIONAL)

- ½ cup sliced almonds
- 1 tablespoon soy sauce or tamari
- 1 tablespoon liquid smoke
- ½ tablespoon pure maple syrup
- ½ teaspoon paprika
- ½ teaspoon kosher salt

FOR SERVING

- 3–4 green onions
- ½ cup sour cream

FOR THE CLASSIC

- Mexican hot sauce (we like Cholula)

FOR THE HOT WINGS

- Cayenne hot pepper sauce (we like Frank's RedHot)
- Blue cheese crumbles

Preheat the oven to 450°F.

Roast the potatoes: Cut the sweet potatoes into ¼-inch slices, leaving the skin on. In a large bowl, mix the sweet potato rounds with the olive oil, garlic powder, chili powder, and kosher salt; stir to thoroughly coat. Line two baking sheets with parchment paper or silicone mats, then place the slices in a single layer on the sheets. Bake 10 minutes on one side, then remove from the oven, flip the slices, and bake another 5 to 7 minutes until tender (but not crisp).

Make the almond bacon (optional): In a small bowl, mix the sliced almonds, soy sauce, liquid smoke, maple syrup, paprika, and kosher salt. Allow to sit for 2 minutes. Spoon the almonds into a large dry skillet, discarding the liquid that remains at the bottom of the bowl. Heat the skillet over medium-low heat and sauté the almonds for 5 to 6 minutes, stirring frequently, until they are sticky and most of the liquid is evaporated. Take care that they do not burn and scrape any sticky bits from the bottom of the pan. When the almonds are sticky and darkened in color, remove them from the heat, spread them onto a plate in a single layer, and allow them to dry until serving, about 10 minutes.

Assemble the rounds: Thinly slice the green onions. When the potatoes are done, remove them from the oven and place them onto a serving plate. To each round, add a small dollop of sour cream and top with sliced green onions. For the Classic, add a dot of Mexican hot sauce. For the Hot Wings, add a dot of Frank's RedHot sauce and 1 crumble of blue cheese. Top all rounds with almond bacon and serve immediately.

GF* For gluten-free, make sure the soy sauce is gluten-free.

V* For vegan, make the classic and omit the sour cream.

Crispy Cumin Chickpeas

GF | V | *Makes 1½ CUPS*

2 15-ounce cans chickpeas
2 tablespoons extra-virgin olive oil
¾ teaspoon kosher salt
2 teaspoons cumin
1½ teaspoons garlic powder
1 teaspoon ground black pepper

Healthy and satisfying, these crunchy bursts are oven-baked with olive oil, cumin, garlic powder, and plenty of black pepper. We like to make up a batch and keep it around for our next salty snack craving; even just a handful are enough to tide us over to a meal. Homemade crispy chickpeas can be difficult to keep from turning soggy after storing: we've tweaked our recipe to make sure these stay crunchy for at least a week. Since the baking time varies based on your oven and the chickpea brand, be watchful in the final minutes of baking.

Preheat the oven to 375°F.

Drain and rinse the chickpeas, then shake off as much remaining water as possible. Place them on a towel on a flat surface; rub your hands over the chickpeas several times, loosening the skins. Quickly remove the loose skins and discard; do this a few times until the majority of the skins are removed (this process should take no more than 5 minutes; you can work quickly and leave a few skins remaining).

In a medium bowl, combine the chickpeas with the olive oil and kosher salt, then add the cumin, garlic powder, and black pepper and stir until fully combined.

Line a baking sheet with parchment paper or a silicone mat and pour the chickpeas onto the sheet, spreading them as far apart as possible. Bake for a total of 50 to 65 minutes, shaking the pan every 15 minutes to ensure the chickpeas bake evenly. The exact baking time depends on the chickpea brand and your oven, so watch closely in the final minutes, taste test, and remove the chickpeas when they are browned and taste crispy but before they become very dark and hard. Allow to cool fully on the baking sheet for about 10 minutes before storing; the chickpeas will crisp up even more as they cool.

Notes

Storage: Store in an airtight container in a dry cupboard for up to 1 week.

A few years ago we hosted a pizza party, and while the pizza was fantastic, everyone kept talking about these olives. They're ripe olives packed in water, which are rich and buttery, not at all like a martini olive. Alex adapted an idea from our favorite Spanish chef José Andrés and marinated them with olive oil, garlic, rosemary, and lemon zest, which brings out a salty earthiness that makes them instantly addictive. Use a mix of green and black olives for visual appeal, and add some fresh rosemary sprigs when serving. We frequently mix up a batch to munch on while we're cooking.

Rosemary Olives

with Lemon Zest

GF | V | *Makes* **1 QUART**

Drain the olives. Peel and thinly slice the garlic. Zest and juice the lemon.

In an airtight container, combine the olives, garlic, lemon zest, lemon juice, olive oil, red wine vinegar, kosher salt, and rosemary sprigs.

Cover and marinate for 2 hours at room temperature.* Serve garnished with additional rosemary sprigs, if desired.

Notes

Storage: Store refrigerated for up to 1 week; allow to come to room temperature before serving.

*If you're short on time, the olives are nearly as good right away.

- 3 6-ounce dry weight cans pitted ripe olives, packed in water (a mixture of green and black in various sizes, not flavored, stuffed, or brined)
- 4 medium garlic cloves
- 1 tablespoon lemon juice plus zest (½ lemon)
- ½ cup extra-virgin olive oil
- 2 tablespoons red wine vinegar
- ½ teaspoon kosher salt
- 4 sprigs rosemary, plus more for serving

Crunchy Dill & Curry Cauliflower Quick Pickles

Pickling is one of those former survival skills that has transformed into a modern day hobby. Since canning can be time consuming, we make quick pickles by simply placing sliced vegetables in a jar with a salty brine mixture. Though quick pickles are not shelf-stable, they can be refrigerated for up to 1 month—and in our experience the jar empties long before that! An overabundance of garden cucumbers prompted us to create our classic dill pickle version. For something a little different, we developed a cauliflower curry pickle that makes a lovely addition to salads or cheese boards (page 57). Both concepts work for whatever vegetables you like, so feel free to get creative. Wide-mouth, 1-quart mason jars work best for packing in as many vegetables as possible.

GF | V | *Makes* **1 QUART EACH**

CRUNCHY DILL PICKLES

6–8 small pickling cucumbers

6 pearl onions or 2 small white onions

6 large sprigs fresh dill

½ tablespoon mustard seeds

½ tablespoon peppercorns

3 medium garlic cloves

1 cup white vinegar

1 tablespoon granulated sugar

2 tablespoons kosher salt

CURRY CAULIFLOWER PICKLES

1 small head cauliflower (about 1½–2 pounds)

1 small or ½ large red onion

3 medium garlic cloves

1 cup white vinegar

2 teaspoons curry powder

1 teaspoon turmeric

1 tablespoon granulated sugar

2 tablespoons kosher salt

Crunchy Dill Pickles

Wash a wide-mouth 1-quart mason jar and its lid in hot soapy water, then rinse and allow to air dry.

Quarter the cucumbers lengthwise. Peel and halve the pearl onions (or quarter the white onions). Holding the jar sideways, tightly pack the cucumbers, onions, and dill sprigs into the jar, sprinkling in mustard seeds and peppercorns as you go and evenly distributing the ingredients.

Peel the garlic. In a small saucepan, combine the garlic, vinegar, 1 cup water, sugar, and kosher salt. Bring to a low boil, stirring occasionally to dissolve the sugar and salt.

Once boiling, pour the brine mixture into the jar, allowing the garlic to settle on top of the vegetables. Tap the jar on the counter to release any air bubbles. Discard any remaining brine, or top off the jar with extra water if any vegetables are exposed at the top. Screw on the lid tightly and allow to cool to room temperature, then store in the refrigerator for at least 24 hours before eating. If desired, discard the garlic after 24 hours.

Curry Cauliflower Pickles

Wash a wide-mouth 1-quart mason jar and its lid in hot soapy water, then rinse and allow to air dry.

Chop the cauliflower into small florets. Peel and thinly slice the red onion. Holding the jar sideways, tightly pack the cauliflower and red onion into the jar, evenly distributing the ingredients.

Peel the garlic. In a small saucepan, combine the garlic, vinegar, 1 cup water, curry powder, turmeric, sugar, and kosher salt. Bring to a low boil, stirring occasionally to dissolve the sugar and salt.

Once boiling, pour the brine mixture into the jar, allowing the garlic to settle on top of the vegetables. Tap the jar on the counter to release any air bubbles. Discard any remaining brine, or top off the jar with extra water if any vegetables are exposed at the top. Screw on the lid tightly and allow to cool to room temperature, then store in the refrigerator for at least 24 hours before eating. If desired, discard the garlic after 24 hours.

Notes
Storage: Store refrigerated for up to 1 month.

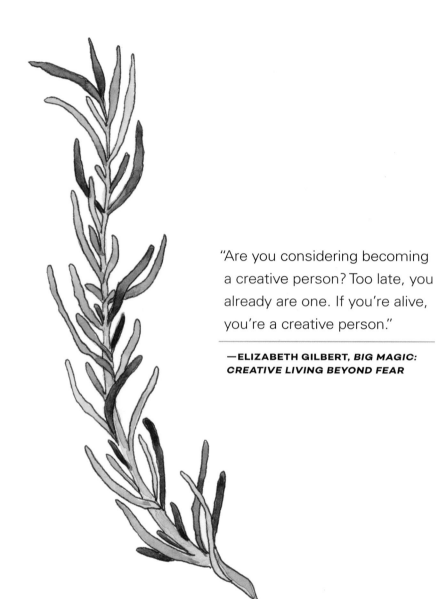

LESSON
03

"Are you considering becoming a creative person? Too late, you already are one. If you're alive, you're a creative person."

—ELIZABETH GILBERT, *BIG MAGIC: CREATIVE LIVING BEYOND FEAR*

Love the (creative) process.

Every human has an inner maker. We all embody a natural desire to be creative. And guess what? We also all need to eat. That means 3 times per day, 21 times per week, and 1,095 times per year we have the opportunity to put something on a plate—and that something can be inspired.

Not every meal has to be creative, but many can be. Dinner can be a chance to try a new spice, make a hearty pasta using only the ingredients on hand, or use leftover kale leaves in a new way. Breakfast waffles can be a canvas for art made with fluffy coconut cream, fresh peaches, and bright green pistachio crumbles. A meal with friends can be a chance to dust off an old cookbook and make an original rendition of empanadas or gnocchi or ceviche.

If you believe cooking is more than just a chore, you'll find it to be rewarding in the best soul-filling kind of way. Make your plate something tasty, interesting, soulful, and intoxicating. Unleash your inner maker.

Salads

Consider this the little black dress of salads. It's versatile enough for an array of occasions and seasons, balancing crisp lettuce, creamy cheese, tart apple, crunchy pistachios, and a sweet-tart honey mustard dressing. We like sprinkling salads with sliced shallots to add a mild onion flavor without the bite of red onion. This loose concept is ripe for creativity: use pears, berries, or sliced roasted beets, walnuts or almonds, and gorgonzola or goat cheese crumbles.

Crisp Green Salad

with Apple & Honey Mustard Vinaigrette

GF | V* | *Serves* 4

FOR THE DRESSING

- 2 **tablespoons Dijon mustard**
- 2 **tablespoons white wine vinegar**
- 2 **tablespoons honey**
- 6 **tablespoons extra-virgin olive oil**

FOR THE SALAD

- 1 **head Bibb lettuce**
- ½ **head frisée (curly endive)**
- 1 **shallot**
- 1 **apple**
- ¼ **cup feta cheese crumbles**
- ¼ **cup chopped pistachios**

Make the vinaigrette: In a medium bowl, whisk together the mustard, white wine vinegar, and honey. Add 1 tablespoon olive oil and whisk until fully combined. Continue adding the remaining olive oil 1 tablespoon at a time, whisking until all 6 tablespoons are added and the dressing is creamy and emulsified.

Prepare the fresh ingredients: Wash and dry the greens and chop or tear them into pieces. Thinly slice the shallot and separate it into rings. Thinly slice the apple (if not serving immediately, mix with a bit of lemon juice to prevent browning).

To serve, place the greens on a plate or in a bowl. Top with the shallot, apple, feta cheese, and pistachios, then drizzle with dressing.

Notes

Storage: Reserve any extra dressing in a sealed container in the refrigerator; bring to room temperature before serving.

Convert this salad to a heartier main dish by topping with hard-boiled eggs and roasted sweet potatoes.

V* For vegan, omit the cheese and substitute maple syrup for the honey.

...rot
...bbon
Salad

with Cumin Lime Vinaigrette

GF | V* | *Serves 4*

Mexican or Latin-inspired meals have become so common in our kitchen that we created this simple side salad to accompany them. Peeling carrots into long ribbons makes them look elegant with minimal effort, and the cumin lime dressing can be whisked together quickly without any chopping or blending. This one usually gets high marks from our dinner guests and is a natural pairing with tortilla soup (page 175), loaded sweet potatoes (page 184), grilled fajitas (page 192), or red and green enchiladas (page 216). Rainbow carrots from the farmers' market add a colorful touch.

FOR THE DRESSING

- 2 **tablespoons lime juice (1 large lime)**
- 2 **teaspoons Dijon mustard**
- 2 **teaspoons honey**
- 1 **teaspoon cumin**
- ¼ **teaspoon chili powder**
- ¼ **teaspoon kosher salt**
- 6 **tablespoons extra-virgin olive oil**

FOR THE SALAD

- 8 **cups mixed baby greens, loosely packed**
- 2 **medium carrots, orange or rainbow**
- 4 **radishes**
- ¼ **cup roasted salted pepitas**
- ¼ **cup feta cheese crumbles (optional)**

Make the vinaigrette: In a medium bowl, whisk together the lime juice, mustard, honey, cumin, chili powder, and kosher salt. Add 1 tablespoon olive oil and whisk until fully combined. Continue adding the remaining olive oil 1 tablespoon at a time, whisking until all 6 tablespoons are added and the dressing is creamy and emulsified.

Prepare the fresh ingredients: Wash and dry the greens and chop or tear them into pieces, if necessary. Peel the carrots into ribbons using a vegetable peeler. Thinly slice the radishes.

To serve, place the greens on plates or in bowls. Top with the carrots, radishes, pepitas, and feta crumbles, then drizzle with dressing.

Notes

Storage: Reserve any extra dressing in a sealed container in the refrigerator; bring to room temperature before serving.

V* For vegan, omit the cheese and substitute maple syrup for honey.

Our travels to the island of Santorini taught us a few things about the famous Greek salad. First, there's no lettuce in a true Greek salad; it's a mix of vegetables based around large, juicy tomato wedges. Kalamata olives and Greek-origin feta round it out, topped with nothing more than olive oil, lemon juice, and a sprinkle of oregano. In Greece, the feta is often served as an entire block that's broken while eating; for this salad, we break ours into crumbles for easy serving. For the best flavor, use only the ripest tomatoes and serve immediately after making.

Classic Greek Salad

GF | **V*** | *Serves 4*

Chop the tomatoes into wedges. Peel the cucumber, cut it in half lengthwise, and then slice the halves into ½-inch-thick half-moon shapes. Peel and thinly slice the red onion. Break the feta cheese into large crumbles.

On a large platter or serving plate, place the tomatoes and sprinkle with a few pinches of kosher salt. Top with cucumbers, red onions, feta cheese, and Kalamata olives. Sprinkle with oregano, then drizzle with olive oil and lemon juice. Serve immediately (do not refrigerate).

Notes
*Save this recipe for when the ripest, juiciest tomatoes are readily available.

For a light dinner, make a Mediterranean spread: pair it with Creamy Artichoke Hummus (page 42), Red Pepper Tabbouleh (page 82), and Baked Pita Crisps (page 61). For a special occasion, pair with Falafel Burgers with Yogurt Dill Sauce (page 212) or Vegetarian Lentil Gyros (page 210).

V* For vegan, omit the feta cheese.

2 large ripe tomatoes (about 1–1½ pounds)*

1 English cucumber

½ small red onion

1 4-ounce feta cheese block (Greek origin, if possible)

2 pinches kosher salt

½ cup pitted Kalamata olives

½ teaspoon dried oregano

2 tablespoons extra-virgin olive oil

2 tablespoons lemon juice (½ large lemon)

Red Pepper Tabbouleh

Tabbouleh was one of the first Mediterranean foods Alex and I discovered together, in a Greek restaurant in a college town in Indiana of all places. It's a refreshing salad made with bulgur wheat, tomato, and lots of lemon and parsley. Here we've re-created our beloved college dish using red pepper instead of tomato. You can serve it as an appetizer with pita or naan (page 122), or as a side dish to Falafel Burgers with Yogurt Dill Sauce (page 212). It doubles easily if you find yourself craving more.

GF* | **V** | *Serves **4 TO 6***

- 1 cup fine-grind bulgur wheat*
- ½ teaspoon kosher salt, plus more as needed
- 1 small red bell pepper
- 3 scallions
- 1 cup finely chopped Italian flat-leaf parsley
- 3-4 tablespoons lemon juice (1 large lemon)
- 2 tablespoons extra-virgin olive oil
- ¼ teaspoon ground black pepper

Make the bulgur: In a heatproof bowl, combine 1 cup boiling water with the bulgur wheat and kosher salt; stir to combine. Cover and allow to sit until the grains are tender and no water remains, about 10 to 15 minutes (or more if necessary).

Prepare the vegetables: Finely dice the red pepper. Thinly slice the scallions. Finely chop the parsley. Juice the lemon.

Assemble the salad: Mix together the bulgur with the vegetables, 3 tablespoons lemon juice, olive oil, and black pepper. Taste and add the remaining tablespoon lemon juice and additional kosher salt as desired. Eat immediately, or let stand for the flavors to meld, noting that the lemon mellows over time.

Notes
Storage: Store refrigerated for 3 to 4 days (if the mixture becomes too dry after refrigeration, mix with a drizzle of olive oil to taste).

*Avoid coarse or extra-coarse bulgur.

GF* For gluten-free, cook 1 cup dry quinoa (page 134); use 2½ cups cooked quinoa as a substitute for the bulgur wheat.

The ruby red confetti snuggled inside a pomegranate must be one of nature's greatest inventions. As two kids who grew up on fruit snacks, when we first shelled a pomegranate Alex and I couldn't quite believe that the seeds grow on trees instead of inside plastic packages! We love eating pom seeds by the handful, but they're also a natural salad topping. This refreshing autumn or winter salad features the sweet, juicy seeds against the crunch of raw fennel and celery, baby greens, and a tangy vinaigrette. It's impressive yet simple to put together, and we like to serve it family-style on a large platter to showcase the vibrant colors.

Fennel, Pomegranate, & Arugula Salad

GF | V | *Serves* 4 TO 6

FOR THE DRESSING

- 1 tablespoon lemon juice (½ lemon)
- 1 tablespoon Dijon mustard
- 2 tablespoons white wine vinegar
- 1 tablespoon honey
- ⅛ teaspoon kosher salt
- 6 tablespoons extra-virgin olive oil

FOR THE SALAD

- 1 pomegranate (½ cup seeds)
- 1 small fennel bulb
- 1 stalk celery
- 6 cups baby spinach and arugula or other baby greens, loosely packed

Make the vinaigrette: Juice the lemon. In a medium bowl, whisk together the lemon juice, mustard, white wine vinegar, honey, and kosher salt. Add 1 tablespoon olive oil and whisk until fully combined. Continue adding the remaining olive oil 1 tablespoon at a time, whisking until all 6 tablespoons are added and the dressing is creamy and emulsified.

Seed the pomegranate: Cut the pomegranate in quarters and place them in a large bowl of water. Under the water, gently pull out the seeds with your fingers. Eventually, you'll be able to turn the peel inside out to extract the seeds closest to the outer skin. As you work, the pomegranate seeds will sink to the bottom, while the white pith from the fruit will float to the top. When all of the seeds are extracted, skim off the white pith and strain out the water. Rinse the pomegranate seeds; reserve ½ cup for the salad and store the extra seeds in a sealed container in the refrigerator for up to 3 days.

Prepare the fresh ingredients: Remove the green fronds from the top of the fennel and thinly slice the bulb. Thinly slice the celery.

Wash and dry the greens as necessary.

To serve, place the greens on a platter. Top with the fennel, celery, and pomegranate seeds. Toss with the desired amount of dressing to taste.

Notes

Storage: Reserve any extra dressing in a sealed container in the refrigerator; bring to room temperature before serving.

Mixed Greens with Peaches

& Balsamic Maple Vinaigrette

Peach season is one glorious month in Indiana. Alex and I make peach salsa (page 50), my mom's custardy peach pie, and caprese salads with peaches and burrata cheese. We also make this side salad as an accompaniment for grilled meals on the patio. It's a summer variation of our Crisp Green Salad with Apple and Honey Mustard Vinaigrette (page 77), starring juicy ripe peaches, crunchy hazelnuts, creamy goat cheese, and bursts of fresh sweet corn, smothered in a maple balsamic vinaigrette. Adding a protein like grilled chicken makes it into a satisfying main dish.

GF | V* | *Serves 4*

FOR THE DRESSING

- 2 tablespoons balsamic vinegar
- 1½ tablespoons pure maple syrup
- 1 teaspoon Dijon mustard
- ¼ teaspoon kosher salt
- Freshly ground black pepper
- 6 tablespoons extra-virgin olive oil

FOR THE SALAD

- 4 cups baby spinach leaves, loosely packed
- 4 cups baby arugula, loosely packed
- 3 small ripe peaches (or 2 large)
- ½ cup fresh corn kernels*
- ¼ cup hazelnuts
- 2 ounces soft goat cheese, crumbled

Make the vinaigrette: In a medium bowl, whisk together the balsamic vinegar, maple syrup, mustard, kosher salt, and several grinds of black pepper. Add 1 tablespoon olive oil and whisk until fully combined. Continue adding the remaining olive oil 1 tablespoon at a time, whisking until all 6 tablespoons are added and the dressing is creamy and emulsified.

Prepare the fresh ingredients: Wash and dry the greens as necessary. Slice the peaches. Cut the corn off of the cob.

Toast the nuts: In a small dry skillet, toast the hazelnuts over medium-low heat until golden and fragrant, stirring frequently and watching carefully, 3 to 5 minutes.

To serve, mix the greens with about half of the dressing and place them on individual plates or in bowls. Top with the peaches, hazelnuts, goat cheese, and corn, and drizzle with the remaining dressing.

Notes

Storage: Reserve any extra dressing in a sealed container in the refrigerator; bring to room temperature before serving.

*For extra flavor, use leftover grilled corn from Grilled Corn with Smoky Paprika Cream (page 106).

V* For vegan, omit the cheese.

Kale Caesar salad is popping up in cookbooks and on restaurant menus alike for good reason—dark green kale leaves are full of nutrients and add a contrasting color and texture to crunchy romaine. Our kale Caesar features a vegan Caesar dressing that uses chickpeas for creaminess, along with some seriously addictive homemade paprika croutons. Look for Tuscan kale, sometimes called Lacinato or dinosaur kale; the color is darker than the standard curly variety, and the flavor is sweeter and more complex.

Kale Caesar Salad

with Paprika Croutons

GF* | V* | *Serves 4 TO 6*

Make the dressing: In a blender, combine the chickpeas, can liquid, lemon juice, dill pickle, mustard, peeled garlic, olive oil, kosher salt, and several grinds of black pepper. Blend on high until smooth and creamy, then taste and add additional salt if desired. Refrigerate until serving.

Preheat the oven to 400°F.

Bake the croutons: Slice the bread into ¾-inch cubes and measure out 3 cups. In a small bowl, mix the bread cubes with the olive oil, paprika, and kosher salt. Spread the bread on a baking sheet in a single layer, then bake for 8 to 10 minutes until golden brown and crisp.

Prepare the fresh ingredients: Wash and dry the romaine hearts and kale. Destem the kale by holding the leaf at the lowest part of the stem and pulling back to tear the leaf away from the stem. Chop both greens into bite-sized pieces.

To serve, place the greens on serving plates or bowls, then top with croutons, dressing, Parmesan cheese shavings (optional), and a sprinkling of lemon zest.

Notes

Storage: Reserve extra dressing in the refrigerator for up to 5 days; bring to room temperature before serving.

GF* For gluten-free, use gluten-free bread.

V* For vegan, omit the Parmesan cheese.

FOR THE DRESSING

- 1 cup chickpeas plus ½ cup can liquid (aquafaba)
- ¼ cup lemon juice (1 large lemon)
- 1 3-inch dill pickle spear or baby dill pickle
- 1 tablespoon Dijon mustard
- 1 medium garlic clove
- ¼ cup extra-virgin olive oil
- ¼ teaspoon kosher salt
- Freshly ground black pepper

FOR THE CROUTONS

- 4 large slices artisan bread
- 1½ tablespoons extra-virgin olive oil
- 1 teaspoon sweet paprika
- ¼ teaspoon plus pinch kosher salt

FOR THE SALAD

- 2 romaine hearts
- 1 bunch Tuscan or Lacinato kale (about 8–12 ounces)
- Parmesan cheese (optional)
- Lemon zest, from the lemon above

Tangy Cucumber & Onion Salad

This refreshing salad is a summer standard in both of our families. My side calls it Gurkensalat, German for cucumber salad. To this day, my mother serves it alongside everything from salmon to burgers. Our version is based on her recipe; it's tweaked for simplicity and adds a pop of fresh dill from our garden.

GF | **V** | *Serves* **6 TO 8**

2 large thin cucumbers, English if possible (about 1½–2 pounds)*

1 small white onion

2 tablespoons chopped fresh dill

½ cup white vinegar

1 tablespoon granulated sugar

1 teaspoon kosher salt

1 teaspoon ground black pepper

Wash the cucumbers and slice them as thinly as possible. Halve the onion and thinly slice it crosswise into half-moon shapes. In a sealable container, combine the cucumbers, onions, and dill.

In a small bowl, mix together the white vinegar, sugar, kosher salt, and black pepper. Pour the vinegar dressing over the vegetables. Mix everything together using your hands to ensure even coverage of the dressing over the vegetables. Cover and refrigerate for at least 1 hour, then stir well again to mix the dressing evenly throughout. Serve using a slotted spoon.

Notes

Storage: Store refrigerated for up to 7 days; the flavor improves over time.

*We prefer using English cucumbers as they have fewer seeds and a lovely green interior; however, any cucumber variety works for this salad.

Pair with Smashed White Bean Salad Sandwiches (page 151) or Giant Portobello Burgers with Caramelized Onions (page 214).

"If you're going to have a sense of fear of failure, you're just never going to learn how to cook. Because cooking is one failure after another, and that's how you finally learn."

—JULIA CHILD

Face your fear.

Cooking, in essence, is risk taking. Whether you're inexperienced or skilled, there's loads of room for failure. Even veteran cooks recognize that the process is humbling. On any given day, the ingredients and distractions might be different, making yesterday's perfect recipe a failure today. The pizza dough might stretch into a lumpy oval, or an accidental extra moment over the heat might overcook the omelet. That's the nature of cooking—it's a variable, human process.

One of the largest obstacles to a home-cooked meal is not simply time or money: it's fear of failure. What if it doesn't work out? What if I mess it up?

In cooking just as in life, failure is part of the process—and it's just as important as success. How you handle (and learn from) the failure is what makes all the difference. So laugh it off, keep the ingredients for a grilled cheese on hand as a backup, and remember that lessons learned the hard way tend to stick. And then roll up your sleeves and jump in.

Side Veg

Broccoli with Feta

GF | **V*** | *Serves 4*

Broccoli has long been maligned, but here's a way to make it sexy: sauté it in olive oil until bright green and tender, then mix with sliced green onions, feta crumbles, and plenty of salt and pepper. It's on the table in 10 minutes and pairs with main dishes both humble and elegant. Or toss it atop a whole grain (page 134) with toasted almonds, a drizzle of Creamy Cashew Sauce (page 142), and lemon zest for a tasty bowl lunch.

2 large heads broccoli (about 1½ pounds)

2 green onions

2 tablespoons extra-virgin olive oil

½ teaspoon kosher salt

¼ teaspoon ground black pepper

3 tablespoons feta cheese

Chop the broccoli into florets. Thinly slice the green onions.

In a 10-inch skillet over medium heat, heat the olive oil. Add the broccoli florets and sauté for 5 minutes, stirring occasionally. Stir in the green onions, kosher salt, and black pepper. Cover and cook for 2 to 3 minutes more, until crisp-tender but still bright green.

Remove the broccoli to a bowl. Top with feta crumbles and additional black pepper or kosher salt to taste. Serve immediately.

V* For vegan, omit the feta cheese.

Lemon & Pepper Green Beans

Since a side dish ideally should be simple to get on the table, our goal with this one was to coax out as much flavor with as little fuss as possible. The beans are quickly pan-steamed in a skillet, then tossed with olive oil, red pepper flakes, lemon, and a hearty sprinkling of black pepper. What remains are some seriously tangy, peppery green beans and only one skillet in the sink.

GF | V | *Serves 4*

1 pound fresh green beans

2 tablespoons lemon juice plus zest (½ lemon)

1 tablespoon extra-virgin olive oil

½ teaspoon red pepper flakes

½ teaspoon kosher salt

Freshly ground black pepper

Remove the ends of the beans. Zest and juice the lemon.

Place the beans in a large skillet with ⅓ cup water, and heat over medium-high heat. Once the water begins to boil, cover the skillet and boil for 4 minutes. Then uncover and cook until the water is fully evaporated.

After the water has cooked out, carefully add the olive oil (since any additional moisture can cause momentary spitting), red pepper flakes, and kosher salt. Sauté, stirring constantly, for 2 minutes more until tender. Turn off the heat and remove the beans to a bowl. Stir in the lemon juice, lemon zest, and several grinds of black pepper. Taste and adjust the flavors as needed.

Notes
Pair with Eggplant Parmesan Casserole (page 183) or The Best Veggie Lasagna (page 218).

Typically we eat edamame with sushi, popping the soybeans out of the shells with our teeth and having too much fun doing it. We've found it's quite simple to make at home, and it makes for an interactive snack or a side for Asian-style dishes like our soba noodle bowls (page 154). The most basic preparation is boiled and sprinkled with salt, but here it's elevated with a touch of toasted sesame oil and a sprinkle of sesame seeds. Make sure to use toasted sesame oil instead of plain, as it lends an earthy, savory fragrance to the dish.

Toasted Sesame Edamame

GF | V | *Serves 4*

Bring a large pot of water to a boil. Boil the edamame until bright green and tender, 4 to 5 minutes, then drain.

Place the edamame in a serving bowl, then mix gently with the sesame oil and sprinkle with the sesame seeds and salt. Add additional salt to taste. Serve warm, with a small bowl for the discarded shells.

Notes

*Do not substitute plain sesame oil for toasted. Sesame oil has a more neutral flavor and is used for cooking and stir frying; toasted sesame oil is a seasoning oil used to add flavor to a dish.

1 pound frozen edamame in the shell
1½ teaspoons toasted sesame oil*
2 teaspoons sesame seeds
¾ teaspoon kosher or fine sea salt

Simple Refried Pinto Beans

These *frijoles refritos* are Alex's creation, a quick side for weeknight meals or a makeshift taco filling. Canned pinto beans are cooked down to a natural creaminess, with some sliced onions added for texture. Instead of the traditional lard, they're pan-fried in a mixture of butter and olive oil, which lends a savory richness. Our meat-loving friends confirm they're a convincing gateway into plant-based eating. Serve them with Huevos Rancheros (page 33) or alongside Mexican or Latin-inspired dishes. Since the brand of canned beans affects the texture, taste, and salt content, you may need to experiment with several brands to find your preference.

GF | V* | *Serves 4*

- 1 small white onion
- 2 15-ounce cans pinto beans
- 1 tablespoon unsalted butter
- 2 tablespoons extra-virgin olive oil
- ½ teaspoon chili powder
- ½ teaspoon kosher salt
- ¼ teaspoon ground black pepper

Halve the onion and thinly slice it into half-moon shapes. Drain the beans, reserving ½ cup of the can liquid.

In a medium saucepan, heat the butter and olive oil over medium heat. Add the onion and sauté until translucent but before it browns, about 3 to 4 minutes. Add the beans, reserved can liquid, chili powder, kosher salt, and black pepper. Turn the heat to medium low and cook for 10 to 15 minutes, stirring often and smashing the beans toward the end of the cook time, until most of the liquid has cooked out and the texture is mashed and thick. Scrape the bottom and sides of the pan as necessary. Taste and season with additional salt as desired, then serve immediately.

V* For vegan, replace the butter with an extra tablespoon of olive oil.

So many of us are scarred from the soggy Brussels sprouts of our childhoods. I wasn't even exposed to them as a child because of the deep-rooted fear developed by my father. But this veggie is making a major comeback, and today, Alex and I have finally convinced our families that crisp-roasted, salty Brussels sprouts are the way to go. Doused in olive oil and sprinkled with kosher salt, they're roasted in a very hot oven so the outer leaves become crispy and blackened. Topping them with shavings of Pecorino, a hard Italian cheese similar to Parmesan, sends them over the top. And if you invest in some Pecorino, it's also the key to our margherita pizza (page 226).

Crispy Brussels Sprouts
with Pecorino

GF | **V*** | *Serves* **4 TO 6**

2 pounds Brussels sprouts

3 tablespoons extra-virgin olive oil

1 scant teaspoon kosher salt

Freshly ground black pepper

Pecorino cheese, for garnish

Preheat the oven to 450°F.

Slice off any hard ends of the sprouts, then slice them in half. In a large bowl, mix them with the olive oil, kosher salt, and several grinds of black pepper.

Line a baking sheet with parchment paper or a silicone mat, then pour the sprouts onto the sheet. Roast for 20 to 25 minutes until blackened and tender (no need to stir).

Serve immediately, garnished with shaved Pecorino cheese.

Notes
Pair with Roasted Acorn Squash with Brown Rice Sausage and Kale (page 206) or Classic Vegetarian Nut Loaf (page 220).

V* For vegan, omit the cheese.

Grilled Corn

with Smoky Paprika Cream

The first thing a Minnesota girl like myself learned moving south was that in Indiana summertime is corn time. Since then, I've learned my favorite method for preparing the golden kernels is placing the husked cob directly onto the grill, which brings out a charred smokiness. When there's time to dress it up, this paprika cream is quick and easy: a bit of yogurt, butter, smoked paprika, and cumin makes for a rich-tasting sauce—and sprinkled with fresh basil, it looks as impressive as it tastes.

GF | **V*** | *Serves 8*

½ cup plain whole milk yogurt

2 tablespoons unsalted butter, melted and slightly cooled

2 teaspoons smoked paprika (pimentón)

1 teaspoon cumin

½ teaspoon kosher salt

8 ears corn

16 fresh basil leaves, for garnish

Heat a grill to medium high.

Make the paprika cream: In a small bowl, mix the yogurt, melted butter, smoked paprika, cumin, and kosher salt.

Grill the corn: Shuck the corn. Place the corn on the grill and cook until it just starts to blacken, then turn and continue cooking and turning until all sides are blackened, 10 to 15 minutes total.

Thinly slice the basil. To serve, spread the paprika cream on the corn and top with the basil.

Notes

Pair with Quick Fix Pinto Bean Tacos (page 156) or Giant Portobello Burgers with Caramelized Onions (page 214).

V* For vegan, substitute ½ cup Creamy Cashew Sauce (page 142) for the yogurt, use 1 tablespoon fresh squeezed lemon juice instead of the butter, and salt to taste.

He caught my eye at the winter farmers' market, a gruff farmer surrounded by hundreds of squashes of every size and color, from enormous blue-gray Hubbards to modest buttercups. The Squash Guy, I dubbed him, and it was he who taught me about delicata squash: a slender, yellow squash with green and orange stripes. In fact, he slipped me a few of this new squash just so I could report back my opinion. I was easily smitten with the variety: since the skin is edible and it roasts fairly quickly, it's simple to prepare—and the taste is sweet and tender. Our best-loved way to eat delicata squash is as fries: roasted half-moon slices that both the kids and adults in our lives rave over. Since the writing of this book, the Squash Guy has sold his Indiana farm and moved on, but he'll always have my heart for the kindness he showed this city girl.

Delicata Squash Fries

with Awesome Sauce

GF | V* | *Serves 4*

Preheat the oven to 450°F.

Roast the squash: Wash the squash. Cut in half lengthwise and scoop out the seeds. Slice into half-moons, about ¼- to ½-inch thick. Place the slices in a bowl and drizzle with olive oil. Add the kosher salt and black pepper and stir to combine.

Line a baking sheet with parchment paper or a silicone mat; place the squash slices on the sheet in a single layer. Roast until tender and slightly browned, about 25 to 30 minutes, depending on the thickness.

Make the sauce: In a small bowl, mix the sour cream, Mexican hot sauce, soy sauce, garlic powder, and dill.

Cool the fries for 2 to 3 minutes before serving; serve warm with dipping sauce.

Notes
Pair with The Ultimate Egg Sandwich (page 152) or White Cheddar Leek and Greens Millet Bake (page 198).

V* For vegan, use Creamy Cashew Sauce (page 142) instead of sour cream.

FOR THE SQUASH
- 3–4 medium delicata squash (2 pounds)
- 1½ tablespoons extra-virgin olive oil
- 1 teaspoon kosher salt
- ½ teaspoon ground black pepper

FOR THE SAUCE
- ½ cup sour cream or crème fraîche (page 139)
- 2 tablespoons Mexican hot sauce (we like Cholula)
- 1 teaspoon soy sauce or tamari (full sodium)
- ¼ teaspoon garlic powder
- ⅛ teaspoon dried dill

Spiced Sweet Potato Wedges

with Chive Cream

One of Alex and my first discoveries in eating real food was that sweet potatoes weren't just for Thanksgiving, topped with lots of marshmallows. Rather than adding more sugar to the naturally sweet vegetable, we favor savory preparations for sweet potatoes—like topped with black beans (page 184) or tossed on a pizza (page 230). This recipe is a simple, everyday way to eat sweet potatoes as a side, roasted with our unique savory spice blend of garlic powder, oregano, and allspice. Serve the wedges with chive cream as a snack, or alongside a vegetarian main, chicken, or fish.

GF | **V*** | *Serves* **4 TO 6**

FOR THE POTATOES

- 1 teaspoon garlic powder
- 1 teaspoon dried oregano
- ½ teaspoon allspice
- 1 teaspoon kosher salt
- 2½ pounds small to medium sweet potatoes
- 2 tablespoons extra-virgin olive oil

FOR THE CHIVE CREAM (OPTIONAL)

- 1 small handful chives
- 1 cup sour cream or crème fraîche (page 139)
- ¼ teaspoon kosher salt

Preheat the oven to 450°F.

Roast the potatoes: In a small bowl, mix the garlic powder, oregano, allspice, and kosher salt.

Wash the sweet potatoes, keeping the skins on. Slice each potato in half crosswise and then in half lengthwise. Place each piece cut-side down and slice it into 3 wedges, for a total of 12 wedges per potato. In a large bowl, mix the potatoes with the spice mix and olive oil.

Line a baking sheet with parchment paper or a silicone mat, and spread the potatoes on the sheet in a single layer. Roast the potatoes for 30 to 35 minutes, until tender and starting to become crisp and browned (no need to stir).

Make the chive cream: Thinly slice the chives and mix them with the sour cream and kosher salt. Taste and add additional salt if desired.

Serve the wedges warm from the oven, along with the chive cream.

Notes

Make ahead/storage: If made in advance and refrigerated, sweet potatoes can be reheated in a 400°F oven for 10 minutes.

V* For vegan, replace the chive cream with Creamy Cashew Sauce (page 142).

Rule #39 in Michael Pollan's manifesto *Food Rules* is that you can eat all the junk food you want, as long as you make it yourself. Hand-cutting fries and baking them at home takes some time, so they're not an every-night sort of indulgence. But we promise that they'll rival the house fries at your favorite restaurant. The secret is using russet potatoes, seasoning them with olive oil, mustard powder, and lots of black pepper, and then baking them in a very hot oven. They're best eaten directly from the oven when they're at their crispiest, served with our lightly sweet homemade honey mustard. Or try them with Awesome Sauce (page 109), Chipotle Aïoli (page 190), Creamy Cashew Sauce (page 142), or Creamy Cilantro Dressing (page 158).

Crispy Baked Restaurant-Style Fries

with Honey Mustard

GF | V* | *Serves 4*

Preheat the oven to 450°F.

Cut the fries: Wash and dry the potatoes, keeping the skins on. Slice off the ends of each potato, and then slice the potato in half lengthwise. Place the potato half cut-side down and cut off a ¼-inch slice lengthwise. Lay the slice on its side and cut it into several long matchsticks (usually about 3, depending on the size of the potato). Repeat until all the potatoes have been cut into fries. The pieces can be uneven in length but aim for a uniform thickness.

Roast the fries: Place the fries in a large bowl and combine with the olive oil, mustard powder, kosher salt, and black pepper. Line two baking sheets with parchment paper or silicone mats, and spread the fries on the baking sheets with as much space between them as possible. Bake for 20 minutes. Remove the trays, flip the fries, and return the trays to the oven, placing each tray on the opposite oven rack. Bake another 15 minutes until the fries are crisp and golden brown, watching closely since the cooking time can depend on your oven and the thickness of the fries. Serve immediately while the fries are crispy; they become softer as they cool.

Make the honey mustard: In a small bowl, mix the Dijon mustard, olive oil, honey, and white wine vinegar. Store refrigerated.

Notes
Storage: To store leftovers, allow the fries to cool to room temperature, then refrigerate or freeze in an airtight plastic bag. Reheat in a 400°F oven for about 5 minutes until warmed through.

V* For vegan, replace the honey with maple syrup.

FOR THE FRIES
- 2½ **pounds russet potatoes (about 6 medium)**
- 2 **tablespoons extra-virgin olive oil**
- 1 **tablespoon mustard powder**
- 1¼ **teaspoons kosher salt**
- 1½ **teaspoons ground black pepper**

FOR THE HONEY MUSTARD
- ¼ **cup Dijon mustard**
- 1 **tablespoon extra-virgin olive oil**
- 1½ **tablespoons honey**
- 1 **teaspoon white wine vinegar**

Turmeric Roasted Cauliflower

When I tell people that roasted cauliflower has the addictive power of popcorn or potato chips, they typically look at me like I've lost my mind. Roasted cauliflower was one of our gateways into cooking whole foods, and back then it seemed ludicrous to use the words addictive and cauliflower in the same sentence. However, roasting this humble vegetable turns it into something entirely different from its raw self: tender, charred, and almost sweet. Here, we've combined it with a few spices and a fresh red Fresno chile pepper, which adds a delicate heat. It's a fantastic side to meat, seafood, or a vegetarian pasta, or as a snack directly from the oven. It's also the star ingredient in our Roasted Cauliflower and Black Bean Tacos with Chipotle Aïoli (page 190).

GF | V | *Serves 4*

- 1 large head cauliflower (about 2 pounds)
- 4 medium garlic cloves
- 1 Fresno chile pepper (or ½ teaspoon red pepper flakes)
- 2 tablespoons extra-virgin olive oil
- 1 teaspoon cumin
- 1 teaspoon paprika
- ½ teaspoon turmeric
- 1 teaspoon kosher salt
- ½ teaspoon ground black pepper

Preheat the oven to 450°F.

Chop the cauliflower into florets. Peel and mince the garlic. If using, remove the seeds from the Fresno chile pepper and slice or mince it. In a large bowl, mix the cauliflower, garlic, and chile pepper with the olive oil, cumin, paprika, turmeric, kosher salt, and black pepper.

Line a baking sheet with parchment paper or a silicone mat, then place the cauliflower in a single layer on the baking sheet. Roast for 25 to 35 minutes until it is tender and browned, stirring once. Serve immediately.

"If you embrace moderation and live within your physical, monetary, and environmental budget rather than constantly exceeding it, you will lose weight, tread more lightly on the planet, and gain satisfaction from these things."

—MARK BITTMAN, *FOOD MATTERS*

Seek balance.

Why is it so easy to overdo something that gives us pleasure? For whatever reason, humans are quick to think that more is better.

Instead of focusing on what not to eat, how about what *to* eat? This allows for wholeheartedly enjoying a humble lentil curry regularly and a rich chocolate cake on occasion. Instead of playing a love-hate game with food, we can reach for home-cooked whole foods not because we should but because they taste so good.

It's easy to feel paralyzed by the "rules" of cooking and eating well. Instead of defining foods as good and evil, using the motto "as much as possible" can bring freedom. Cook whole foods as much as possible, eat as many vegetables as possible, and buy organic, local, and sustainable where possible. In some life seasons, as much as possible might not be a lot. But instead of living out of guilt for what we're not doing, we can create a sustainable practice by celebrating each step in the right direction.

And then, of course, make a day to break all the rules.

Baked

Corn Muffins

with Green Onions

My sister and I grew up on Jiffy Corn Muffin Mix, and that enticing blue box is seared in my memory. We were always elated when muffins were on the dinner menu, and my sister would sneak bites of the batter from the bowl. Here's Alex and my from-scratch take on the classic corn muffin: moist, lightly sweet from maple syrup, and balanced with the right amount of salt. The secret to avoiding the infamous cornbread dryness is yogurt, which keeps it fluffy and light. We've also added sliced green onions for a savory counterpoint. The muffins bake in the time it takes to simmer a stew and pair with everything from a soup to a summer barbecue to a main dish salad.

GF* | **V*** | *Serves* **12**

2–3 green onions

1⅓ cups yellow cornmeal

⅓ cup whole wheat flour

⅓ cup all-purpose flour

2 teaspoons baking powder

¼ teaspoon baking soda

1 teaspoon kosher salt

2 eggs

4 tablespoons unsalted butter, melted and slightly cooled

1 cup plain whole milk yogurt

½ cup 2% milk

¼ cup pure maple syrup

Preheat the oven to 400°F. Line a 12-cup muffin tin with paper liners.

Thinly slice the green onion tops and measure out ⅓ cup. In a large bowl, mix the cornmeal, whole wheat flour, all-purpose flour, baking powder, baking soda, and kosher salt. In a small bowl, whisk together the eggs, then mix in the melted butter, yogurt, milk, and maple syrup.

Pour the liquid ingredients into the dry ingredients and mix until just combined. Fold in the green onions.

Pour the batter into the paper liners. Bake 13 to 15 minutes until puffed and golden, and a toothpick inserted in the center of a muffin comes out clean. Remove from the pan and serve warm or at room temperature.

Notes

Storage: Store in an airtight container for up to 2 days at room temperature or refrigerated. Or, freeze in an airtight plastic bag for up to 2 weeks.

Serve with Chipotle Black Bean Tortilla Soup (page 175), Darn Good Vegan Chili (page 179), or Big Mexican Salad with Creamy Cilantro Dressing (page 158).

GF* For gluten-free, use gluten-free flour.

V* For vegan, omit the eggs. In place of the butter, yogurt, and milk, use 5 tablespoons grapeseed oil, 1 teaspoon apple cider vinegar, and ¾ cup almond milk. Pour into 8 muffin cups and bake about 15 minutes.

Homemade Whole Wheat Naan

Alex and I use this chewy, soft Indian flatbread for everything from dipping into curry to standing in for pizza crust. It's cooked in a hot cast-iron skillet to mimic the traditional tandoor oven. Serve it with an Indian-style curry (page 188), alongside a main dish salad, as the base of a naan pizza,* or in Chickpea Shawarma Flatbread (page 148). Our recipe uses whole wheat flour, which adds a nutty flavor. It's a bit of a project, so make it with friends and family when time allows. Naan saves well, so you can make it in advance and keep leftovers at room temperature or frozen.

Makes 8 LARGE NAAN

2½ cups all-purpose flour

1½ cups whole wheat flour

2¼ teaspoons instant yeast

2 teaspoons baking powder

2 teaspoons plus pinch kosher salt, divided

6 tablespoons unsalted butter, divided

1 cup 2% milk

½ cup full-fat Greek yogurt

2 tablespoons honey

2 medium garlic cloves

Italian flat-leaf parsley, for garnish (optional)

Mix and knead the dough (15 minutes): In a mixing bowl, combine the all-purpose flour, whole wheat flour, yeast, baking powder, and 2 teaspoons kosher salt. Melt 2 tablespoons butter. Add the milk, yogurt, honey, and melted butter to the mixing bowl, and stir until a loose dough forms. If necessary, add an extra splash of milk to bring the dough together. Turn the dough onto a floured counter and knead until it is stretchy and smooth, about 7 to 8 minutes.

Let the dough rise (about 2 hours): Place the dough back into the bowl and cover it with a clean towel. Allow the dough to rise in a warm spot until doubled in size, about 1 to 2 hours depending on the environment. When the dough has doubled, punch it down. Divide the dough into 8 equal-sized balls. Cover and allow to rest another 15 minutes.

Cook the naan (about 20 minutes): When ready to cook the naan, peel and mince the garlic. Place 4 tablespoons butter in a small saucepan and add the garlic; cook over low heat until the butter is melted.

Heat a large skillet over medium heat (cast iron works best if you have it). Prepare a bowl of water and a pastry brush. On a lightly floured counter, roll one dough ball into an oval about 6 inches to 7 inches long and ¼-inch or less thick. Brush one side of the naan lightly with water and place wet-side down in the hot skillet; lightly brush the top with water. Quickly cover with a lid and cook until dark brown to black splotches form, 1 to 2 minutes. Flip and press down to deflate any bubbles, and cook another 1 to 2 minutes until cooked through and slightly blackened in parts. Remove from the skillet and brush liberally with melted garlic butter.

Continue for all remaining naan, adjusting the heat as necessary to ensure even cooking. Place the finished naan on a tray in a 250°F oven and serve warm. If desired, sprinkle the naan with chopped parsley and a pinch of kosher salt.

Notes

Storage: To store, allow the naan to cool fully, then place in an airtight plastic bag and keep at room temperature for up to 3 days or freeze for up to 2 months. Reheat frozen naan by wrapping it in aluminum foil and baking in a 350°F oven for 15 minutes.

*Naan pizza: Preheat the oven to 450°F. Place the naan directly on the oven grate and bake 3 minutes on each side. Remove from the oven, add the desired toppings, and bake again until the cheese is melted, about 5 minutes.

Multigrain Sandwich Loaf

Alex is the bread baker in our household. He'll swear to you that the smell of fresh baked bread makes all the planning, mixing, and waiting worth the while. This loaf he created as an everyday sandwich bread: nutty and moist, it's full of fiber and whole grains and doesn't contain the preservatives that keep store-bought bread shelf stable. As with our pizza dough (page 224) and Crusty Multigrain Artisan Bread (page 126), the rhythm of baking takes some practice but becomes more intuitive with time.

Makes **2 LOAVES**

¼ cup honey

¼ cup unsalted butter, melted

2½ cups warm water

1½ tablespoons instant yeast*

1 tablespoon kosher salt

3 cups whole wheat flour

2 cups bread flour**

1 cup rye flour

1 cup rolled oats

Mix and knead the dough (15 minutes): In a large bowl, combine the honey, melted butter, warm water, yeast, and kosher salt, and mix with a wooden spoon. Add the whole wheat flour, bread flour, rye flour, and oats to the bowl and stir again until just combined. Turn the dough out onto a clean, lightly floured countertop.

Using your hands, start to form the dough into a ball. At first it will be rather floury, then after about 30 seconds it will become quite sticky. Resist the urge to add too much extra flour unless the stickiness is unbearable. Knead the dough by repeatedly pushing it with the base of your palm; continue kneading for 8 to 10 minutes.

Let the dough rise (2 to 3 hours): Return the dough to the bowl and cover it with a clean dish towel. Allow the dough to stand in a warm place until it rises to double its size, about 1 to 2 hours.

Once the dough has risen, grease two standard-sized loaf pans with oil or butter. Turn the dough onto a counter and divide it into two equal parts. Gently press each dough into a large rectangle about ½-inch thick. The short side of each rectangle should be about the same length as the long edge of the loaf pan.

Starting from the short side of the rectangle, gently roll the dough into a log, then place it into the pan seam-side down. Gently press the dough to fill the bottom of the pan. Repeat for the second loaf. Score the top of the loaves multiple times with a sharp knife and sprinkle them with oats, then gently press the oats into the top of the bread. Cover with a clean dish towel and allow to rest for 45 minutes.

Bake the bread: Preheat the oven to 375°F.

Bake the loaves for 35 to 40 minutes, turning the pans once for an even bake. At 25 minutes, spray the tops of the loaves evenly with

water using a spray bottle, which makes for a dark and hard crust. The loaves are done when they sound hollow when tapped, or the inside of the bread measures 190°F on a thermometer. Allow to cool several minutes in the pans, then remove the loaves from the pans and allow them to finish cooling on a rack before eating, at least 30 minutes.

Notes

Storage: To store, allow the bread to cool completely, then keep at room temperature for 1 to 2 days wrapped in a towel to allow it to breathe. Slice off anything you don't plan to eat in the next few days (it's helpful to preslice), wrap it in plastic wrap, and store it in the freezer; allow it to come to room temperature prior to serving.

*Buying yeast in a jar and storing it in the freezer allows it to stay fresh indefinitely. The yeast can be used straight from the freezer.

**Bread flour is different from all-purpose flour; it is a high-protein flour that helps to create more rise in yeasted breads.

Crusty Multigrain Artisan Bread

My dad baked bread regularly before I was born, but it slipped away once life got busy with raising children and work. Now a granddad, he resurrected the hobby when Alex and I shared with him a simple no-knead method by a friend of ours, Zoë François. Zoë developed this recipe with her friend Jeff Hertzberg to make homemade bread accessible to everyone, and their book *Artisan Bread in Five Minutes a Day* quickly became wildly popular. Alex and I modified her recipe into a multigrain version, adding whole wheat and rye flours and mixing a handful of seeds into the dough. When my dad came to visit upon the birth of our son Larson, he and I honed the recipe further, adding black sesame seeds for an even nuttier flavor and an egg wash for a glossy finish. There's nothing quite like the smell of fresh-baked bread, and my dad is now solidly back in the habit.

V* | *Makes* **2 LARGE LOAVES**

¼ cup rolled oats
¼ cup quinoa
¼ cup sunflower seeds
2 tablespoons black sesame seeds
¼ cup cold water
1 tablespoon instant yeast*
1½ tablespoons kosher salt
3 cups lukewarm water
4 cups all-purpose flour
1 cup rye flour
1 cup whole wheat flour
1 egg white plus 1 tablespoon water
2 cups warm water

Soak the add-ins (1 hour): In a small bowl, stir together the oats, quinoa, sunflower seeds, black sesame seeds, and cold water. Let stand for 1 hour.

Mix the dough and let it rise (about 2 hours): In a large mixing bowl, combine the yeast and salt, then add the lukewarm water and mix well. Using a large wooden spoon or dough whisk, gradually mix in the flours and the soaked oats and seeds. Mix only enough to combine; do not knead or overwork the dough. Cover with a towel, place on a counter at room temperature, and allow the dough to rise for 2 hours.

Chill the dough (12 hours to 1 week): Cover the bowl with plastic wrap, place it in the refrigerator, and allow it to rest for at least 12 hours or up to 1 week. It can be baked any time in the next week; you can bake the two loaves on different days, or bake both loaves on the same day and freeze one of them.

Rest and bake the bread (1½ hours): Preheat the oven to 450°F, placing a pizza stone on the middle rack. (If desired, you can bake it on a baking sheet, but we recommend a pizza stone for the crispiest crust.) On a lower rack, place an old sheet pan and for maximum steaming effect, add lava rocks to the pan.** Since you'll be pouring water onto the pan, it's helpful to push the stone to one side of the oven so that there is space for pouring.

Sprinkle a pizza peel or baking sheet with cornmeal. Divide the dough in half (if baking one loaf, leave the dough for the second loaf in the bowl and refrigerate it until baking). Sprinkle the dough and your hands with just enough flour to keep the dough from

sticking, then gently shape it into a loaf by stretching the edges down and under the loaf and pinching it together. Place the loaf with the pinched-side down on the cornmeal-dusted peel, cover with a clean dish towel, and allow it to rest for 40 minutes.

After the rest is complete, in a small bowl, mix the egg white with the water. Use a sharp knife to cut several ½-inch-deep slashes at an angle along the top of the loaf. Then gently brush the top with the egg wash.

Slide the loaf onto the pizza stone and close the door. (If baking two loaves at once, place them as far apart as possible so they don't touch as they bake.) Prepare 2 cups of warm water in a liquid measuring cup. Wearing an oven mitt, open the oven door. Carefully and quickly pour the water onto the sheet pan to create steam (look away to make sure the steam does not hit your face). Close the door immediately.

Bake for 40 to 45 minutes until brown and crispy or until the bread has an internal temperature of 205°F; the loaf should sound hollow when tapped. Remove the bread from the oven and cool it on a rack, about 2 hours.

Notes

Storage: To store, allow the bread to cool completely, then keep at room temperature for 1 to 2 days wrapped in a towel to allow it to breathe (alternatively, sliced bread saves for a few days at room temperature wrapped in aluminum foil in an airtight plastic bag). For longer term storage, slice off anything you don't plan to eat in the next few days (it's helpful to preslice), wrap it in plastic wrap, and store it in the freezer; allow it to come to room temperature prior to serving.

*Buying yeast in a jar and storing it in the freezer allows it to stay fresh indefinitely. The yeast can be used straight from the freezer.

**Lava rocks can withstand high heat and their irregular shape creates loads of steam when they come into contact with water. Lava rock is available in the grilling section in hardware stores.

V* For vegan, omit the egg wash.

"People cannot change their habits without first changing their way of thinking."

—MARIE KONDO, *THE LIFE-CHANGING MAGIC OF TIDYING UP*

Be mindful.

It's easy to go on autopilot: to drive without looking, talk without thinking, and eat without tasting. Mindfulness is the opposite: being fully aware of the present moment.

Eating mindfully is a thoughtful way to approach food. It's tasting each bite. Instead of balancing plates in front of a screen or eating on the run, it's sitting down at a table. It's intentionally indulging in chocolate mousse with friends instead of sneaking spoonfuls late at night in front of the refrigerator. It's eating off a plate instead of compulsively snacking from a bag. It's investing in quality ingredients and buying from the best sources. It's slicing fresh basil leaves to top your homemade pizza.

Approaching food with mindfulness can sound impossible and lofty. Mindful eating is not an easy practice, and there's certainly no call for perfection. However, little by little, slowing down and approaching our plates with care can grow an awareness that over time can be life changing.

From Scratch

DIY Dried Beans

Cooking dried beans isn't exactly a necessity for the modern home cook, since canned beans are readily available. However, like making bread (page 124), it feels good in a homesteading way. It's also cheaper: one pound of dried beans makes the equivalent of four cans of beans. Home-cooked beans have a lovely taste and texture, especially if you add herbs, onions, or garlic while simmering. The magic conversion factor for canned versus dried: one 15-ounce can of beans equals 1½ cups cooked beans. Freezing the beans in 1½-cup portions makes for easy use.

1 **pound dried beans of any type**
   Kosher salt*

Rinse the dried beans and pick out any debris or broken pieces. Place the beans in a sealable container, cover them with water, and place them in the refrigerator to soak overnight.

When ready to cook, pour the beans into a large pot, and cover with water at least 1 inch above the top of the beans. Bring to a simmer but do not boil.

Simmer gently, uncovered and stirring occasionally, for 30 minutes to 1 hour, depending on the variety. As a reference, black and cannellini beans take about 1 hour, and pinto and chickpeas take about 45 minutes. The beans are done when they are tender but not mushy. Note that varieties of beans cook to different textures; some tend fall apart more than others when cooking.

Once tender, add kosher salt to the cooking water until the water tastes seasoned. Allow the beans to cool. Store them in their cooking liquid for up to 3 days in the refrigerator or freeze them for later use.

Notes

Storage: Freeze in 1½ cup portions (equal to a 15-ounce can), along with the cooking liquid. If freezing in canning jars, fill the liquid to about two-thirds of the jar to allow for expansion in the freezer. To defrost, pull a jar from the freezer and allow to defrost for several hours in the refrigerator, or microwave if desired.

For a ready-to-eat side dish, we recommend seasoning the beans by adding aromatics such as peeled garlic, peeled onions, or fresh herbs (tied together with kitchen twine) during boiling.

*Do not add salt to your beans while cooking, which may cause them to break apart.

Perfect Grains:

Quinoa, Brown Rice, Bulgur, Farro, & Freekah

Eating whole grains can be a lot more interesting than just a sandwich made with whole wheat bread. You can eat these grains with a curry or stew, as the basis for a bowl meal with raw or roasted veggies and a sauce (page 200), or with chopped fresh herbs as a side. These are the five whole grains most likely to end up on our table. We typically boil 1½ cups of the dry whole grain to make 4 servings. We've found that when you're eating a meal of mostly vegetables, it's nice to have a substantial amount of a filling grain on hand, especially for big appetites.

Quinoa
Water to grain ratio **2 TO 1**

Why we like it: It's quick cooking and gluten-free, and the texture is light and fluffy. Since it can have a slightly bitter taste, make sure to rinse before cooking and season well after cooking.

Featured in: Moroccan Sweet Potato Stew (page 196)

GF | **V** | *5 cups cooked; serves* **4**

- 1½ cups quinoa
- 3 cups water
- Kosher salt

Using a strainer, rinse the quinoa under cold water, then drain it completely.

Place the quinoa in a saucepan with the water. Bring it to a boil, then reduce the heat to low. Simmer where the water is just bubbling for about 17 to 20 minutes, until the water has been completely absorbed (check by pulling back the quinoa with a fork to see if water remains). If necessary, stir once to incorporate any uncooked grains on the top.

Remove from the heat, then cover the pot and allow the quinoa to steam for 5 minutes. Uncover and fluff the quinoa with a fork.

To serve, season with kosher salt to taste.

Brown Rice

Water to grain ratio **6 TO 1**

Why we like it: While it takes a bit longer to prepare than white rice, it contains more nutrients and pairs well with everything from Mexican to Indian cuisines. The "pasta method" avoids the risk of soggy rice.

Featured in: Turmeric Rice Bowls with Lemon Tahini Drizzle (page 200), Burrito Bowl with Cumin Lime Crema (page 187)

GF | **V** | *5 cups cooked; serves* **4**

- 1½ cups long or short grain brown rice*
- 9 cups water
  Kosher salt

Using a strainer, rinse the rice under cold water, then drain it completely.

In a saucepan over high heat, bring the water to a boil. Add the rice, stir once, and continue to boil uncovered for 30 minutes, bubbling rapidly. Taste a grain of rice; if it is tender, remove the pan from the heat and pour the rice into the strainer.

Return the rice to the pot (without the heat). Cover the pot and allow the rice to steam for 5 to 10 minutes. Uncover and fluff the rice with a fork.

To serve, season with kosher salt to taste.

Notes

*For white rice, use the same method and boil for about 10 minutes, until tender.

Leftover rice can become very dry. To reheat it, add the rice to a saucepan with a splash of water. Cover the rice and steam it over low heat for a few minutes, stirring occasionally, until the rice is heated through. Remove the heat and let sit for a few minutes to steam before serving.

Bulgur Wheat

Water to grain ratio **1 TO 1**

Why we like it: It's quick to make and can be prepared with nothing more than a teapot and a bowl.

Featured in: Red Pepper Tabbouleh (page 82), Santorini Bowls (page 163)

V | *5 cups cooked; serves* **4**

- 1½ cups fine- or medium-grind bulgur wheat*
- 1½ cups boiling water
  Kosher salt

Boil the water (a tea kettle works well). In a heatproof bowl, combine the boiling water and bulgur wheat; stir to combine. Cover and allow to sit until tender: 7 minutes for fine-grind bulgur and 15 minutes for medium-grind bulgur.

To serve, season with kosher salt to taste.

Notes

*Do not use coarse or extra-coarse bulgur with this method. For coarse-ground bulgur, follow the package instructions.

Farro

Water to grain ratio **6 TO 1**

Why we like it: It's chewy, satisfying, and cooks in much less time than a similar more common grain, barley. Using the "pasta" method (similar to brown rice on page 136) makes for reliable results across varying brands.

Try it: Use in a grain bowl with veggies and a sauce (page 200), or mixed with roasted vegetables, olive oil, and balsamic vinegar.

V | *5 cups cooked; serves* **4**

- 1½ cups pearled farro*
- 9 cups water
  Kosher salt

In a saucepan over high heat, bring the water to a boil. Add the farro, stir once, and continue to boil uncovered for about 20 minutes, bubbling rapidly. Taste a grain of farro; if the grain is plump and tender, remove the pan from the heat and pour it into a strainer. If not, continue to cook and taste until tender. Brands of farro can vary, so adjust the cook time as necessary.

To serve, season with kosher salt to taste.

Notes
*Semipearled farro has more of the fiber and nutrient-rich bran intact, which gives it more nutritional value. You can use the recipe above; it simply takes longer to boil than pearled farro. If the package does not specify pearled or semipearled, simply cook until tender using the method above.

Freekah

Water to grain ratio **3 TO 1**

Why we like it: It's unique and nutty; lighter than farro but closer in texture to bulgur.

Try it: Use as an alternative to rice for Red Lentil Coconut Curry (page 188) or Cauliflower Curry (page 176) or in a grain bowl with veggies and a sauce (page 200).

V | *5 cups cooked; serves* **4**

- 1½ cups freekah
- 4½ cups water
  Kosher salt
  Freshly ground black pepper

In a saucepan, combine the freekah and water and bring it to a boil. Reduce the heat to a simmer and cook uncovered for 15 to 17 minutes, stirring occasionally, until the freekah is tender and the liquid is completely absorbed.

Remove from the heat, cover, and let stand to steam for 5 minutes.

To serve, season with kosher salt and freshly ground black pepper to taste.

Crème fraîche (pronounced krem fresh) is a French cream some-where between sour cream and whipped cream. It's velvety thick and can be used in any way you'd typically use sour cream. Making it at home is a bit of a science experiment: mix heavy cream and yogurt together, then let it sit for 1 to 2 days on a countertop while it thickens from the natural culture of the yogurt. The bacteria in the cream aids in preservation, making it safe to sit at room tempera-ture. We make it at home because it can be hard to find, and it's a DIY experiment that's satisfying every time. The uses are endless: mix it with chopped chives as a dip for roasted vegetables or add a dollop over fruit or a dessert (page 251). Since it doesn't separate or curdle when heated, it's ideal for topping soups and stews; it's also the magic ingredient in our "best" veggie lasagna (page 218).

Crème Fraîche

GF | *Makes* **2 CUPS**

1 pint (2 cups) heavy whipping cream
2 tablespoons plain yogurt

In a glass or plastic sealable container, stir together the cream and yogurt. Cover and let sit at room temperature for 36 to 48 hours, until it becomes very thick. (The mixture won't spoil on the counter, since the acid in the mix prevents bacteria associated with dairy products.)

Notes
Storage: Stores in the refrigerator for up 2 weeks and will continue to thicken while refrigerated.

Super Sauces

Contrary to classic French cooking where sauces are complicated and labor intensive, we find ourselves drawn to sauces that can bring intense flavor with simple preparation. Although each sauce in this book is given with a specific recipe, all can be mixed and matched. Serve any of them with fish, chicken, or roasted potatoes, as a dip for vegetables, or drizzled over vegetables and grains in a bowl meal.

DRIZZLING SAUCES

Salsa Verde (page 172): Stews, fish, or as a dip for bread.

Romesco (page 37): Potatoes, asparagus, with fish or poultry.

Cilantro Chutney (page 188): Curries, fish, or on a sandwich.

Cumin Lime Crema (page 187): Tacos or a dip for veggies.

Lemon Tahini Drizzle (page 200): Bowl meals or veggie burgers.

Creamy Cashew Sauce (page 142): Bowl meals, stews, baked potatoes, or on a sandwich.

Creamy Caesar Dressing (page 89): Salads, bowl meals, or a dip for veggies.

Creamy Cilantro Dressing (page 158): Salads, bowl meals, or a dip for fries or veggies.

DIPPING SAUCES

Yogurt Dill Sauce (page 212): Veggie burgers or a dip for veggies or pita.

Chipotle Aïoli (page 190): Tacos, a dip for roasted potatoes, or on avocado toast.

Honey Mustard Sauce (page 113): Potatoes or on a sandwich.

Awesome Sauce (page 109): Good on just about everything.

Chive Cream (page 110): Potatoes, on a bagel, or a dip for veggies.

Creamy Cashew Sauce

GF | V | *Makes* **1 CUP**

Simply blending cashews with broth and salt makes for a creamy, savory sauce that mimics the texture of sour cream or yogurt. It's vegan and dairy-free without any tradeoffs in flavor. Drizzle the sauce over bowl meals or whole grains (page 134), or even spread it on bread as an alternative mayo. We've provided ideas for a few other variations: try it green by adding cilantro, or Mexican style with adobo sauce, cumin, and lime.

- 1¼ cups raw unsalted cashews
- ¾ cup vegetable broth (or water)
- ½ teaspoon kosher salt, plus more to taste

Place the cashews in a bowl and cover them with water. Soak for 1 hour, then drain.

Add all ingredients to a blender, and blend on high for 1 minute. Stop, scrape, and add additional liquid if necessary to come to a creamy consistency. Blend for several minutes until creamy and smooth. If desired, add additional salt to taste.

Notes

Storage: Store in a sealed container in the refrigerator for up to 1 week or in the freezer for several months.

Green variation: Blend with a few handfuls of cilantro and a squeeze of lime. Taste and adjust flavors as desired.

Mexican-style variation: After blending, mix ½ cup Creamy Cashew Sauce with a few teaspoons adobo sauce (from 1 can chipotle peppers in adobo sauce), ¼ teaspoon cumin, and a squeeze of lime juice, to taste.

"Never forget: This very moment,
we can change our lives. There
never was a moment, and never
will be, when we are without the
power to alter our destiny."

—STEVEN PRESSFIELD,
THE WAR OF ART

Yes, you can.

Just as each of us is creative, deep down every human has a small, nagging voice. You're not good enough. You're a failure. You'll never learn. Meet your inner critic, that voice in your head that judges and demeans, making you feel bad, inadequate, worthless, and guilty. The inner critic can be a massive obstacle to embracing nutritious ingredients and maintaining a positive relationship with food. It's no wonder we sneak into the kitchen for ice cream then criticize ourselves into a guilty mess, or resort to takeout one night and stop cooking altogether.

Home cooking and wholesome eating is bound to frustrate the inner critic. It's simply doing its job, trying to protect us from failure. But to embrace new patterns, we've got to see the inner critic for what it is.

After acknowledging the inner critic exists, we can practice self-compassion, replacing those negative messages with positive statements of truth about what we can do. Because even though the inner critic demands it, there is no need for perfection. Instead, we can strive to do our best today—and remember there is always room tomorrow to try again.

Mains
Simplest Fare

Chickpea Shawarma Flatbread

GF* | *Serves 4*

This one is for stressed mamas and dads, single guys or ladies who don't cook, or anyone looking for a quick fix that's more than just a sandwich. Flatbread has often saved us when we're looking for a speedy bite that's classy enough to be called dinner. With Mediterranean-spiced chickpeas, creamy hummus, and a quick version of our yogurt dill sauce (page 212), this flatbread is so flavorful it even works for guests, paired with a salad and a glass of wine. If you enjoy Mediterranean flavors and have time to spare, try some of our traditional Greek mains: Falafel Burgers (page 212) or Vegetarian Lentil Gyros (page 210).

- 1 cup (7 ounces) plain whole milk Greek yogurt
- 1 tablespoon chopped fresh dill or ½ teaspoon dried dill
- 1¼ teaspoons garlic powder, divided
- 1 teaspoon kosher salt, divided
- 2 15-ounce cans chickpeas
- 1 teaspoon ground cumin
- 1 teaspoon paprika, plus more for garnish
- ⅛ teaspoon cinnamon
- ⅛ teaspoon red pepper flakes
- 1 teaspoon freshly ground black pepper
- 2 tablespoons extra-virgin olive oil
- 4 whole wheat naan or pita*
- 1 cup hummus*
- 1 handful cilantro, for garnish

Make the yogurt sauce: In a small bowl, stir together the Greek yogurt, dill, ¼ teaspoon garlic powder, ¼ teaspoon kosher salt, and 3 to 4 tablespoons water until a loose sauce forms. Taste, and add a few more pinches kosher salt as necessary.

Sauté the chickpeas: Drain and rinse the chickpeas; shake off as much water as possible. In a small bowl, combine 1 teaspoon garlic powder with the cumin, paprika, cinnamon, red pepper flakes, black pepper, and ¾ teaspoon kosher salt. In a large skillet, heat the olive oil over medium heat. Add the chickpeas and spices and sauté, stirring frequently, until warm and the chickpeas are evenly coated with spices, about 4 to 5 minutes.

To serve, spread each naan or pita bread with the hummus, then top with warm chickpeas, yogurt sauce, torn cilantro leaves, and a sprinkle of paprika. Using a pizza cutter, slice each flatbread into 4 pieces.

GF* For gluten-free, use gluten-free naan or pita.

*If you have time to spare, use Homemade Whole Wheat Naan (page 122) and Creamy Artichoke Hummus (page 42).

This vegetarian play on tuna salad relies on white beans as the base. The beans become so creamy when smashed that only a touch of mayonnaise is needed to bring it together, and celery seed and tangy lemon juice intensify the flavor. It's ultra versatile: slather it on thick bread slices as a sandwich, mound it on top of salad greens, or spread it on a croissant for an impressive brunch. In the summer, we add chopped basil, chives, or tarragon for an herby kick. It's unassumingly tasty, and we make it for quick lunches or dinner in a pinch.

Smashed White Bean Salad Sandwiches

GF* | **V*** | *Makes **2 SANDWICHES***

Thinly slice the celery and green onions. Drain and lightly rinse the navy beans.

In a medium bowl, roughly smash the beans with a fork, leaving about a third of them whole. Stir in the celery, green onions, mayonnaise, lemon juice, celery seed, garlic powder, kosher salt, and several grinds of black pepper. Taste and continue adding kosher salt a few pinches at a time until the flavor pops but is not too salty; the exact amount of salt will vary based on the brand of beans.

Toast the bread. Thinly slice the radishes. Place lettuce on one slice of bread, then spread the bean salad. Top with sliced radishes and the remaining slice of bread.

Notes
Storage: Store white bean salad refrigerated until serving.

GF* For gluten-free, use gluten-free bread.

V* For vegan, use vegan mayonnaise or substitute 1 to 2 tablespoons Creamy Cashew Sauce (page 142) for the mayonnaise, to taste.

1 stalk celery

3 small green onions

1 15-ounce can navy or cannellini beans

1 tablespoon mayonnaise

2 tablespoons lemon juice (½ lemon)

¾ teaspoon celery seed

⅛ teaspoon garlic powder

¼–½ teaspoon kosher salt

Freshly ground black pepper

4 slices bread or 2 croissants

2 radishes

2 leaves lettuce

The Ultimate Egg Sandwich

As kids, my sister and I always loved when our mom decided to scrap the pot roast and just make egg sandwiches for dinner. Something about it not being a "real" dinner made it infinitely more fun. Now as adults, egg sandwiches have become a real dinner for Alex and me on evenings where we need something quick because they're simple, filling, and so delectably good. Here's our ultimate egg sandwich: a runny yolk, silky, smoky mayonnaise, juicy tomato, and thick crusty bread. It's simple, but the combination of textures and flavors elevate it to almost gourmet status.

GF* | *Serves 4*

¼ cup mayonnaise

2 teaspoons Mexican hot sauce (we like Cholula)

2 teaspoons smoked paprika (pimentón) or ½ teaspoon liquid smoke

1 large ripe tomato

1 avocado

2 leaves romaine lettuce

8 slices whole grain country bread

½ tablespoon unsalted butter

4 eggs

Kosher salt

Freshly ground black pepper

In a small bowl, mix together the mayonnaise, hot sauce, and smoked paprika or liquid smoke.

Slice the tomato and avocado. Tear the romaine leaves in half. Toast the bread.

In a large skillet, melt the butter over medium heat. Add the eggs and sprinkle with a few pinches of kosher salt and several grinds of black pepper. Cook for 2 to 3 minutes, until the whites are firm (do not flip).

To serve, top one bread slice with lettuce, tomato, a pinch of kosher salt, avocado, and egg. Spread the other slice of bread with smoky mayo and place it on top of the sandwich. Serve immediately.

GF* For gluten-free, use gluten-free bread.

Rainbow Soba Noodle Bowls

Smothered in a creamy Asian-inspired sauce, noodles are just one of the components in this beautiful bowl full of veg. A rainbow of raw carrots, cabbage, cucumber, radishes, and green onion provide a fresh contrasting crunch to the savory umami of the noodles. The vegetables here are simply suggestions, so customize to your own preferences—then garnish with sesame seeds, lime juice, and spicy sambal oelek. While it looks stunning, it's pretty simple to pull together. Serve it with Toasted Sesame Edamame (page 101).

GF* | V | *Serves 4*

12 ounces soba noodles

4 medium garlic cloves

1 2-inch nub fresh ginger

2 cups vegetable broth

6 tablespoons peanut butter

1 tablespoon flour

2 tablespoons pure maple syrup (or honey)

6 tablespoons soy sauce, divided

2 tablespoons lime juice, plus lime wedges for serving (2 limes)

2 tablespoons toasted sesame oil

4 green onions

3 radishes

¼ small red cabbage

4 carrots

1 cucumber

8 cups baby spinach leaves, loosely packed

Sesame seeds, for serving*

Sambal oelek or Sriracha, for serving

Cook the noodles: Start the water to boil and cook the noodles according to the package instructions while preparing the remaining ingredients. When the noodles are finished, drain them, rinse with cool water, and leave them in a colander.

Make the sauce: Peel the garlic and ginger. In a blender, combine the garlic, ginger, broth, peanut butter, flour, maple syrup, and 2 tablespoons soy sauce. Purée on high until fully combined and a thin sauce forms.

Juice the lime. In a small bowl, mix the lime juice with the toasted sesame oil and ¼ cup soy sauce; set aside.

Prepare the vegetables: Thinly slice the green onions, radishes, and red cabbage. Peel the carrots and julienne them into thin strips (using a julienne peeler is handy). Julienne the cucumber: cut the cucumber in half crosswise and slice off the rounded ends. Stand one half on end and cut thin slices down the length of the cucumber. Remove the curved side slices, lay the remaining slices down flat, and thinly slice long ribbons. Repeat with the other half of the cucumber. Slice the remaining lime into wedges for a garnish and set aside.

Finish the noodles: When the noodles are cooked, return the empty noodle pot to the stove; add the peanut sauce and spinach and bring it to a simmer. Simmer for about 2 minutes until the sauce thickens and the spinach is fully wilted. Turn off the heat, add the noodles and stir, then stir in the soy-lime juice mixture.

To serve, artfully arrange the noodles and vegetables in large, shallow bowls, and top with sesame seeds, a bit of sambal oelek or Sriracha (to taste), and a squeeze of lime juice.

Notes

Storage: Refrigerate any leftovers. The noodles save well, and the sauce stays creamy after chilling.

Additional topping ideas include sliced avocado, bean sprouts, shredded kale, glazed tempeh (page 200), cilantro, and roasted Brussels sprouts (page 105).

*If time allows, toast the sesame seeds in a dry skillet over medium heat for 3 to 5 minutes until lightly browned and fragrant, stirring occasionally.

GF* For gluten-free, use gluten-free noodles (like rice noodles) and ½ tablespoon cornstarch in place of the 1 tablespoon flour.

Quick Fix Pinto Bean Tacos

Tacos are where we head when we're not sure what's for dinner, and these can be whipped up in minutes. When Alex first made me this filling, I was skeptical about the egg and bean combination. But after tasting it he won me over. It's surprisingly satisfying; the eggs provide a chewy, almost meaty texture, and the chili powder and cumin bring just enough savory spice. Purple cabbage slivers tossed with lime and salty feta crumbles make for a simple, contrasting topping. For especially hungry eaters, it's easy to double the filling. If you're in the mood for tacos and have more time to spare, try our Roasted Cauliflower and Black Bean Tacos with Chipotle Aïoli (page 190).

GF | *Makes **8 TACOS***

1 small white onion

1 15-ounce can pinto beans

1 cup corn kernels, fresh or frozen (optional)

2 tablespoons lime juice (1 lime)

2 cups thinly sliced red cabbage

2 tablespoons extra-virgin olive oil, divided

1 teaspoon kosher salt, divided

2 eggs

1 teaspoon chili powder

1 teaspoon cumin

1 teaspoon garlic powder

8 corn tortillas

2 cups baby spinach leaves or other baby greens, loosely packed

½ cup feta cheese crumbles

Mexican-style hot sauce, for serving

Prepare the vegetables: Peel and mince the onion. Drain and rinse the pinto beans. Cut the corn off of the cob or warm frozen corn to room temperature (if using).

Marinate the cabbage: Juice the lime. Thinly slice the red cabbage, then mix it with the lime juice, 1 tablespoon olive oil, and ¼ teaspoon kosher salt.

Cook the beans and eggs: Heat 1 tablespoon olive oil in a 10-inch skillet over medium heat. Add the onion and sauté for about 3 to 4 minutes until translucent. Crack the eggs into the skillet and cook with the onion, stirring constantly until the eggs are scrambled into small pieces and just set, about 2 minutes. Add the beans and stir to combine, then stir in the chili powder, cumin, garlic powder, and ¾ teaspoon kosher salt. Cook for about 3 minutes until warmed through.

Char the tortillas: If desired, char the tortillas by turning on a gas burner to medium heat and placing the tortilla directly on the grate. After about 15 seconds when the edges are lightly charred, use tongs to flip the tortilla and heat on the opposite side until lightly charred. Repeat for all tortillas, taking care that they do not catch fire.

To serve, place the spinach on the tortillas, then top with the beans, red cabbage, feta crumbles, corn, hot sauce, and additional toppings as desired.

Notes
For dairy-free, omit the feta cheese.

xican Salad

with Creamy Cilantro Dressing

GF | V | *Serves 4*

On busy weeknights, Alex and I like to throw a bunch of vegetable odds and ends on a plate and call it a meal. This main dish salad is based on one of our throw-together meals and features a tangy green cilantro dressing that relies on chickpeas for creaminess. Loading the salad with black beans, chickpeas, pepitas, and feta crumbles makes it a hearty vegetarian main that's pretty simple to put together. You can use any vegetables you have on hand but make sure to balance with proteins like beans, seeds, nuts, and cheese to keep it filling—or try topping it with sautéed shrimp or chicken. For a hearty meal, serve it with a side of avocado toast, Corn Muffins with Green Onions (page 120), or Handmade Tortilla Chips (page 58) and Roasted Poblano Salsa (page 49).

FOR THE DRESSING

- 1 medium garlic clove
- 4 green onions
- 3 tablespoons lime juice (about 1½ limes)
- 1 cup packed cilantro leaves and tender stems, plus more for garnish
- ¾ cup canned chickpeas plus ¼ cup can liquid or water*
- 1 tablespoon Dijon mustard
- 1 teaspoon honey
- ¼ cup extra-virgin olive oil
- 1 teaspoon ground cumin
- ½ teaspoon kosher salt

FOR THE SALAD

- 5 radishes
- 1 red bell pepper
- 1 Fresno chile pepper (optional)
- ¾ cup fresh corn kernels
- 3 large romaine hearts
- 1 avocado (optional)
- 1 15-ounce can black beans
- ¾ cup chickpeas*
- 2 teaspoons extra-virgin olive oil
- ¾ teaspoon kosher salt
- ⅓ cup roasted salted pepitas

Make the dressing: Peel the garlic. Chop the dark and light green portions of the green onions into 3-inch chunks; reserve the white portions for the salad. Juice the limes. In a blender, combine the garlic, green onions, lime juice, cilantro, chickpeas, can liquid, mustard, honey, olive oil, cumin, and kosher salt. Blend on high until smooth and creamy; taste and add additional lime juice or kosher salt if desired. Reserve and refrigerate until using.

Prepare the vegetables: Thinly slice the white portions of the green onions. Thinly slice the radishes. Seed and dice the red pepper. Seed and thinly slice the Fresno chile pepper, if using. Cut the corn off of the cob. Chop the romaine into bite-sized pieces. Chop the avocado, if using.

Prepare the beans: Drain the black beans. In a medium bowl, mix the beans with the chickpeas, olive oil, and kosher salt.

To serve, place the romaine in bowls, then top with the vegetables and beans. Garnish with pepitas and torn cilantro leaves, drizzle with dressing, and serve.

Notes

Storage: Reserve any extra dressing in a sealed container in the refrigerator for 1 to 2 days; bring to room temperature before serving.

*The chickpeas in the dressing plus the chickpeas in the salad amount to one 15-ounce can.

Use leftover dressing as a dip for chips, roasted potatoes, or veggies.

Kale &
Goat Cheese
Rigatoni

Our friend Amy transformed an urban parking lot into an organic farm; she's one of the hardest working people we know—and she always has the dirt under her fingernails to prove it. Her booth at the farmers' market is always mounded high with drop-dead gorgeous produce: multicolored radishes, beets, turnips, and always loads of greens. This recipe is for her waving rows of kale: a simple, flavorful weeknight pasta that's elegant enough to serve for guests. Tangy goat cheese becomes a creamy binder for pasta studded with garlic and shallots. It works with any short pasta shape (twisted torcetti is fun if you can find it), garnished with bright lemon zest and a sprinkling of freshly ground black pepper.

GF* | *Serves 4*

- 1 tablespoon (for the pasta water) plus 1 teaspoon kosher salt, divided
- 1 pound rigatoni or torcetti, penne, or orecchiette, whole wheat if possible
- 1 bunch Tuscan or Lacinato kale (about 8–12 ounces)*
- ¼ cup extra-virgin olive oil, divided
  Freshly ground black pepper
- 4 medium shallots
- 4 medium garlic cloves
- 1 teaspoon red pepper flakes
- 4 ounces soft goat cheese
  Zest of 1 lemon

Cook the noodles: Bring a large pot of water to boil with 1 tablespoon kosher salt. Once boiling, add the pasta and cook until al dente (according to the package instructions), then drain.

Sauté the kale: Destem the kale by holding the leaf at the lowest part of the stem and pulling back to tear the leaf away from the stem, then roughly chop the leaves. In a large skillet, heat 1 tablespoon olive oil, then add the kale and sauté over medium-high heat until bright green and wilted, about 3 minutes. Remove from the heat and stir in ¼ teaspoon kosher salt and several grinds of black pepper, then place in a serving bowl. Wipe out the skillet.

Sauté the shallot and garlic: Thinly slice the shallots into rings, enough for 1 cup. Peel and mince the garlic. In the same skillet, heat 3 tablespoons olive oil over medium heat, then add the shallot and sauté until sizzling and translucent, about 2 minutes. Add the garlic and red pepper flakes and stir for 30 seconds until fragrant, then remove from the heat.

Combine the ingredients: In a serving bowl, combine the kale with the drained pasta, shallots, and garlic, then add dollops of goat cheese and ½ teaspoon kosher salt. Mix gently to combine. Taste and add an additional ¼ teaspoon kosher salt if desired.

To serve, place the pasta on plates or serving bowls. Garnish each serving with grated lemon zest and several grinds of black pepper.

Notes
*Use any type of green in place of kale, including chard, collard greens, or spinach.

GF* For gluten-free, use gluten-free pasta.

Santorini, a volcanic island in Greece, is like a dream. We'd seen hundreds of photographs before we visited, but being there was almost too good to be true: crystal blue water for miles and white stucco abodes baking under the impossibly bright sun. This bowl was inspired by the clean flavors we found on our Mediterranean adventures: fresh parsley, briny olives, and salty feta, contrasted with cool cucumber and juicy tomato. Fine grain bulgur wheat is traditional in Greece and requires no "cooking": it's simply mixed with boiling water and left to stand until the grains are plump. Drizzled with a lemony vinaigrette, it makes for a simple but inspired bowl meal.

Santorini Bowls

GF* | **V*** | *Serves 4*

Make the bulgur: Prepare the bulgur wheat (page 136). When it is tender, mix it with the kosher salt.

Make the chickpeas: Drain and rinse the chickpeas, and shake them dry. Zest the lemon. In a small bowl, mix the chickpeas with the lemon zest, olive oil, kosher salt, and several grinds of black pepper.

Make the vinaigrette: In a medium bowl, whisk together the lemon juice, white wine vinegar, mustard, and kosher salt. Add 1 tablespoon olive oil and whisk until fully combined. Continue adding the remaining olive oil 1 tablespoon at a time and whisking until all 6 tablespoons are added and the dressing is creamy and emulsified.

Prepare the vegetables: Thinly slice the shallots into rings. Slice the tomatoes in half and the cucumber into slices; sprinkle them with a bit of kosher salt.

To serve, place the salad greens into large, wide bowls. Top with bulgur wheat, shallots, tomato, cucumber, chickpeas, and Kalamata olives. Sprinkle the entire bowl with feta crumbles, torn parsley leaves, and lemon vinaigrette. If desired, add a dollop of hummus. Serve with pita wedges or crisps.

Notes

GF* For gluten-free, substitute quinoa for the bulgur wheat (page 134).

V* For vegan, omit the feta cheese.

FOR THE BULGUR

- 1½ cups fine or medium-grind bulgur wheat
- ½ teaspoon kosher salt

FOR THE CHICKPEAS

- 1 15-ounce can chickpeas
- Zest of ½ large lemon
- 1 tablespoon extra-virgin olive oil
- ¼ teaspoon kosher salt
- Freshly ground pepper

FOR THE VINAIGRETTE

- 1 tablespoon lemon juice (from the ½ lemon above)
- 1 tablespoon white wine vinegar
- 1 teaspoon Dijon mustard
- ¼ teaspoon kosher salt
- 6 tablespoons extra-virgin olive oil

FOR THE BOWL

- 2 shallots
- 1 pint ripe cherry tomatoes
- 1 small cucumber
- 8 cups chopped mixed greens
- ½ cup sliced Kalamata olives
- ½ cup feta cheese crumbles
- 1 handful Italian flat-leaf parsley
- 1 dollop hummus, purchased or Creamy Artichoke Hummus (page 42) (optional)

Tuscan White Bean & Fennel Soup

One of the first recipes Alex and I created together was an Italian white bean soup using fennel and chard from our winter farmers' market. The fennel had an unexpected savoriness, and Alex added a hint of smoked paprika for an earthy depth. We called it pizza soup; it's one of the recipes from the beginning of our food journey that we still make to this day. The San Marzano variety of canned tomatoes is best if you can find it; it's an Italian tomato variety that we also use on our pizzas (page 226). If you can't find it, use the highest quality canned tomato you can find, even fire roasted. And while it's not required, shavings of Pecorino cheese make for a lovely garnish.

GF | **V*** | *Serves 6*

- 1 fennel bulb
- 4 medium garlic cloves
- 2 15-ounce cans cannellini beans
- 1 bunch Tuscan or Lacinato kale (about 8–12 ounces)*
- 2 tablespoons extra-virgin olive oil
- 1 28-ounce can San Marzano diced tomatoes (or other high-quality tomatoes)
- 1 15-ounce can San Marzano diced tomatoes
- 1 bay leaf
- 1 quart (4 cups) vegetable broth
- ½ teaspoon red pepper flakes
- 1 teaspoon dried basil
- 1 teaspoon smoked paprika (pimentón)
- 1 teaspoon kosher salt
- Freshly ground black pepper
- Pecorino or Parmesan cheese, for garnish (optional)

Remove the stems from the fennel bulb and cut off any tough parts from the bottom of the root, then dice the remaining bulb. Reserve some green sprigs for a garnish. Peel and mince the garlic. Drain and rinse the cannellini beans. Destem the kale by holding the leaf at the lowest part of the stem and pulling back to tear the leaf away from the stem, then roughly chop the leaves.

In a large pot or Dutch oven, heat the olive oil over medium-high heat. Add the fennel and sauté for 4 minutes, until translucent but not browned. Reduce the heat to medium, add the garlic, and sauté for 30 seconds.

Carefully add both cans of tomatoes and their juices, then add the bay leaf and simmer for 5 minutes.

Add the vegetable broth and cannellini beans and bring to a boil. Once boiling, reduce to a simmer and add the kale, red pepper flakes, basil, smoked paprika, kosher salt, and several grinds of black pepper. Simmer until the kale is tender, about 5 minutes. Remove and discard the bay leaf, then taste and adjust flavors as necessary. To serve, garnish with fennel sprigs and grated cheese if desired.

Notes

*Tuscan kale is sometimes called Lacinato or dinosaur kale; the color is darker than the standard curly variety, and the flavor is sweeter and more complex.

Pair with Crusty Multigrain Artisan Bread (page 126) and a salad.

V* For vegan, omit the cheese.

Stew sounds like something that's simmering all day long, but these red lentils cook up in minutes. Red lentils are naturally split so they cook faster than standard lentils, and they're full of nutrients and fiber. This stew is loaded with smoked paprika (trust us, 2 tablespoons is no typo!), which has hit the mark with meat lovers in our lives. A squeeze of lemon, torn cilantro, and tangy Greek yogurt make for a bright garnish. Make a double recipe when serving hungry eaters, or serve over rice or another whole grain for a more filling dish.

Smoky Red Lentil Stew

GF | V* | *Serves 3 TO 4*

Peel and finely dice the carrots and onion, then finely dice the celery. Peel and mince the garlic.

In a large pot or Dutch oven, heat the olive oil over medium heat. Add the onion, carrots and celery, and sauté until the onion is translucent, about 5 to 6 minutes.

Add the garlic and sauté for 1 minute. Then stir in the balsamic vinegar, smoked paprika, cumin, cayenne, and lentils and stir for another minute. Add the broth, kosher salt and a few grinds of black pepper. Bring to a low simmer, then cover halfway and gently simmer until the lentils are just soft but before they start to break apart, about 7 to 10 minutes. Watch closely and taste to assess doneness. The finished soup should be brothy with the lentils just soft; cooking past this point yields a very thick stew (which is just as delicious but less soup-like). Stir in the lemon juice.

To serve, ladle the soup into bowls. Garnish with torn cilantro or parsley leaves, Greek yogurt, and a sprinkle of smoked paprika.

Notes
Pair with Corn Muffins with Green Onions (page 120), Homemade Whole Wheat Naan (page 122), or Crusty Multigrain Artisan Bread (page 126).

V* For vegan, omit the Greek yogurt and use Creamy Cashew Sauce (page 142).

- 2 **large carrots**
- 1 **medium yellow onion**
- 2 **stalks celery**
- 3 **medium garlic cloves**
- 3 **tablespoons extra-virgin olive oil**
- 1 **tablespoon balsamic vinegar**
- 2 **tablespoons smoked paprika (pimentón), plus more for garnish**
- ¼ **teaspoon cumin**
- ¼ **teaspoon cayenne**
- 1¼ **cups red lentils**
- 1 **quart (4 cups) vegetable broth**
- ¾ **teaspoon kosher salt**
  Freshly ground black pepper
- 2 **tablespoons lemon juice (½ large lemon)**
- 1 **handful cilantro or Italian flat-leaf parsley, for garnish**
  Plain Greek yogurt, for garnish (optional)

"There is nothing better than putting a plate of delicious food on the table for the people you love."

—ALICE WATERS, *IN THE GREEN KITCHEN*

Gather and share.

Everything about a meal is meant to be shared, from the first sizzle of the onions meeting the oil to the final morsel of apple cardamom crumble. When food is shared, magic happens. Inviting a stranger to the table is almost a guarantee that they'll leave as a friend.

Cooking and eating naturally connects us to others. If you're looking to cook more, invite a friend, partner, or spouse into the process. Cook with your children. Have friends over and instead of making dinner before they come, cook it together. Spend Sunday afternoon on a crusty loaf of bread and a simmering pot of soup, and invite the neighbors over for an evening of laughter and a bottle of wine.

To care about food is to care about people. At the table, we can learn to appreciate our differences and expand our minds and palates to cultures from all over the globe. In fact, scientific studies confirm that eating the same food around the table increases people's sense of trust and cooperation—further proof that sharing food with one another unites us.

Mains
Everyday Favorites

Artichoke Lentil Stew

with Salsa Verde

This salsa verde is not the traditional Mexican green salsa but the lesser-known Italian version, a zesty lemon–garlic–parsley–caper sauce. We jokingly call it sexy sauce for its bright garlicky goodness. As a base, this hearty springtime stew is a play in contrasts: light green peas, asparagus, and artichokes pair with dark earthy kale and lentils. The end result is a thick stew that pairs well with a crusty bread (page 126) or corn muffins (page 120). You'll want to make salsa verde again and again—drizzle it over roasted cauliflower or grilled fish, or use it as a dip for bread.

GF | **V** | *Serves 4*

FOR THE STEW

- 1 large yellow onion
- 1 large carrot (or 2 small)
- 3 medium garlic cloves
- ½ bunch Tuscan or Lacinato kale (about 4 ounces)*
- 8 thick or 12 thin asparagus stalks (or substitute an additional 1 cup snow peas)
- 1 cup snow peas
- 3 tablespoons extra-virgin olive oil
- 1 tablespoon dried oregano
- 1 tablespoon dried basil
- 1 bay leaf
- 1 quart (4 cups) vegetable broth
- 1 15-ounce can quartered artichoke hearts, drained
- 1 cup dried green lentils
- 1 teaspoon kosher salt, plus more to taste
- Freshly ground black pepper

FOR THE SALSA VERDE

- ¼ cup chopped Italian flat-leaf parsley
- Zest of ½ lemon
- 1 small garlic clove
- 1 tablespoon jarred capers
- 6 tablespoons extra-virgin olive oil
- ¼ teaspoon kosher salt
- Freshly ground black pepper

Make the stew: Peel and dice the onion and the carrot. Peel and mince the garlic. Destem the kale by holding the leaf at the lowest part of the stem and pulling back to tear the leaf away from the stem, then chop the leaves into roughly bite-sized pieces. Chop the asparagus and peas into bite-sized pieces, removing any tough stems from the peas if necessary.

In a large pot or Dutch oven, heat the olive oil over medium heat. Add the onion and carrot and sauté until tender, about 5 minutes. Add the garlic, oregano, basil, and bay leaf and sauté for about 1 minute until the garlic is fragrant. Add the broth, artichoke hearts, lentils, kale, kosher salt, and several grinds of black pepper. Bring to a simmer and gently cook for 10 minutes until the lentils are tender but still hold their shape. Add the asparagus and cook 5 minutes more. Add the peas and cook another 3 minutes until bright green and tender. When the stew is done, remove the bay leaf; it will be thick and stew-like, not brothy. Taste and add a pinch or two of additional salt if desired.

Make the salsa verde: Meanwhile, finely chop the parsley. Zest the lemon. Peel and mince the garlic. Drain and finely chop the capers. In a small bowl, mix the parsley, lemon, garlic, capers, olive oil, kosher salt, and several grinds of black pepper.

To serve, ladle into large shallow bowls and top with generous spoonfuls of salsa verde.

Notes
*Use any type of green in place of kale, including chard, collard greens, or spinach.

Our version of tortilla soup features black beans and a secret ingredient: adobo sauce packed in a can of chipotle peppers. It's our trick for adding a smoky background flavor to Mexican cuisine (see pages 190, 192, and 216). In this soup, it brings warmth without being spicy. Combined with crunchy tortilla strips, radishes, and plenty of lime, the flavors are fitting for a weeknight meal or a game-day gathering. Quality tortillas are key; for best results, use thin, authentic-style corn tortillas that are pliable and not too dry.

Chipotle Black Bean Tortilla Soup

GF* | **V** | *Serves* **4 TO 6**

Preheat the oven to 375°F.

Make the tortilla strips: Brush the tortillas lightly with olive oil on each side. Using a pizza cutter, slice them in half, then into thin strips. Place the strips on a baking sheet and sprinkle with kosher salt. Bake for 10 to 12 minutes until crispy and lightly browned.

Make the soup: Peel and dice the onion. Dice the green pepper. Peel and mince the garlic. Drain and rinse the beans.

In a large pot or Dutch oven, heat 2 tablespoons olive oil and sauté the onion until translucent, about 5 minutes. Add the green pepper and the garlic and sauté for 2 minutes. Stir in the oregano and the cumin for 1 minute. Add the tomatoes, beans, corn, adobo sauce, broth, and kosher salt. Bring to a boil, then simmer for 10 minutes. Taste and add additional adobo sauce or kosher salt if desired.

Prepare the garnishes: Slice the radishes. Slice the lime into wedges.

To serve, ladle the soup into bowls and allow to cool to warm. Garnish with the tortilla strips, radishes, torn cilantro leaves, hot sauce, and plenty of lime juice.

Notes
*Use 1 tablespoon adobo sauce from the can; the peppers and remaining sauce can be reserved (or frozen) for future use.

Pair with Corn Muffins with Green Onions (page 120) or Carrot Ribbon Salad with Cumin Lime Vinaigrette (page 78).

GF* For gluten-free, use gluten-free adobo sauce (check packaging prior to purchase).

- 6 6-inch corn tortillas
- 2 tablespoons extra-virgin olive oil, plus more for brushing
- 1 teaspoon kosher salt, plus more for sprinkling
- 1 yellow onion
- 1 green bell pepper
- 4 medium garlic cloves
- 2 15-ounce cans black beans
- 2 teaspoons dried oregano
- 1 teaspoon cumin
- 1 28-ounce can crushed tomatoes
- 1½ cups frozen corn (fire roasted, if possible)
- 1 tablespoon adobo sauce (from 1 can chipotle peppers in adobo sauce)*
- 1 quart (4 cups) vegetable broth
- 1 teaspoon kosher salt
- 4 radishes, for garnish
- 1 lime, for garnish
- 1 handful cilantro, for garnish
- Hot sauce (optional)

Creamy Cauliflower Cashew Curry

with Pickled Onions

A good curry is comforting and homey; this one is inspired by a dish made for us by dear friends on a dark winter evening. Both vegan and gluten-free, the creamy sauce is a blend of onion, garlic, ginger, and coconut milk. Crunchy pickled onions add a tart complement and a splash of color. Curry blends vary widely, so don't be afraid to try a few before you land on one you love—just be sure to use a high-quality curry powder since it significantly affects the overall flavor. The curry pairs well with naan (page 122).

GF | V | *Serves 4*

FOR THE PICKLED ONIONS

- ½ medium red onion
- 3 tablespoons apple cider vinegar
- 1 tablespoon honey or granulated sugar
- ¼ teaspoon ground coriander
- ¾ teaspoon kosher salt

FOR THE CURRY

- 2 cups uncooked white or brown basmati rice
- 1 yellow onion
- 4 medium garlic cloves
- 1 1½-inch nub fresh ginger
- 4 large carrots
- 1 large head cauliflower (about 2 pounds)
- 2 tablespoons extra-virgin olive oil
- 1 15-ounce can full-fat coconut milk*
- 2 tablespoons curry powder
- ¼ cup yellow raisins
- ½ cup cashew halves
- 1¼ teaspoons kosher salt
  Freshly ground black pepper
- 4 cups baby spinach leaves, loosely packed (chopped if leaves are large)
- 1 handful cilantro, for garnish

Make the pickled onions: Peel and thinly slice the red onion into crescent shapes, slicing from the top end to the root end, enough for 1 cup. In a small bowl, whisk together the apple cider vinegar, honey, coriander, kosher salt, and ½ cup warm water. Add the onions and let stand at room temperature for 30 minutes to one hour (the longer the better).

Cook the rice (page 136).

Make the curry: Peel and chop the yellow onion into quarters. Peel the garlic. Peel the ginger and slice it into rounds. Peel the carrots and slice them into thin rounds. Cut the cauliflower into bite-sized florets, removing the stems as much as possible. Reserve the carrots and cauliflower in a bowl.

Use a food processor to combine the onion, garlic, and ginger and blend until smooth.

Over medium-high heat in a large Dutch oven or pot, heat the olive oil, then add the blended ingredients. Cook for 5 minutes until fragrant, stirring frequently to make sure that it does not brown. Then add the coconut milk and curry powder and cook for 2 minutes, stirring until smooth. Add the carrots, cauliflower, raisins, cashews, 1 teaspoon kosher salt, and several grinds of black pepper. Cover and cook for 15 minutes until the cauliflower is tender, occasionally uncovering and stirring to mix the sauce with the vegetables. Stir in the spinach leaves, cover and cook until wilted, about 3 minutes. Taste and add an additional ¼ teaspoon kosher salt, if desired.

To serve, spoon the curry over rice and garnish with pickled onions and torn cilantro.

Inspired by a chili cook-off, our vegan chili features a blend of vegetables to thicken the chili and bulgur wheat to mimic the traditional meaty texture. We've left a blank slate in terms of spice level so that it can be customized to taste with hot sauce. Somehow this big pot of vegetables can hold its own against a traditional chili—and the leftovers taste even better.

Darn Good Vegan Chili

GF* | **V** | *Serves* **6 TO 8**

Chop the parsley.

In a blender, blend the 15-ounce can of tomatoes, carrot (roughly broken into a few pieces), parsley, and Worcestershire sauce until fully combined into a thick, reddish-brown paste.

Peel and dice the onion. Dice the green pepper and the celery. Drain the beans. In a large pot or Dutch oven, heat the olive oil over medium-high heat. Add the onion, green pepper, and celery, and sauté for 5 to 6 minutes until tender.

Carefully add the blended vegetables, two 28-ounce cans tomatoes, beans, bulgur wheat, chili powder, garlic powder, onion powder, cumin, oregano, kosher salt, and black pepper. Simmer gently for 20 to 25 minutes until the chili thickens slightly and the bulgur is tender, stirring occasionally. Serve with garnishes as desired.

Notes
Pair with Corn Muffins with Green Onions (page 120).

GF* For gluten-free, use quinoa.

- 1 cup chopped Italian flat-leaf parsley
- 1 15-ounce can petite diced tomatoes
- 1 small carrot
- 2 tablespoons vegan Worcestershire sauce
- 1 large yellow onion
- ½ green bell pepper
- 2 ribs celery
- 1 15-ounce can pinto beans, drained
- 1 15-ounce can kidney beans, drained
- 2 tablespoons extra-virgin olive oil
- 2 28-ounce cans petite diced tomatoes
- ½ cup bulgur wheat or quinoa
- 3 tablespoons chili powder
- 1 tablespoon garlic powder
- 1 teaspoon onion powder
- 1 teaspoon ground cumin
- 1 teaspoon dried oregano
- 1½ teaspoons kosher salt
- ¼ teaspoon ground black pepper
- Creamy Cashew Sauce (page 142) , for serving
- Hot sauce, for serving

Creamy Vegan Potato Chowder

Chowders are typically loaded with bacon and cream; this one has neither but is still creamy and bold. We'll give away our tricks: cashews blended with some of the simmered soup make a creamy body, and a blend of spices, garlic, and soy sauce simulate the umami of meat. Neither Alex nor I eat solely vegan, but we love the challenge of inventing satisfying plant-based options to cook for others. For the garnish, thin strands of chard and sliced green onions bring an unexpected crunch. The soup involves a bit of chopping up front, but the end result is worth it.

GF* | **V** | *Serves 4*

- ½ cup unsalted raw cashews
- 1 large Vidalia onion
- 2 carrots
- 3 ribs celery
- 2 medium garlic cloves
- 2 pounds russet potatoes (about 5 medium size)
- 2 tablespoons extra-virgin olive oil
- 6 cups vegetable broth
- 2 tablespoons soy sauce
- 1 teaspoon paprika
- 1 teaspoon dried thyme
- 1 teaspoon dried oregano
- 1 teaspoon onion powder
- ½ teaspoon garlic powder
- ¾ teaspoon kosher salt, plus more to taste
- ½ teaspoon ground black pepper
- 1½ cups corn, fresh or frozen
- 2 green onions, for garnish
- 2 large chard leaves, for garnish

Place the cashews in a bowl and cover them with cold water; allow them to soak while preparing the recipe.

Peel and dice the onion and carrots, then dice the celery and place them together in a bowl. Peel and mince the garlic, and peel and dice the potatoes.

In a large pot or Dutch oven, heat the olive oil over medium-high heat. Sauté the onion, carrots, and celery for 2 minutes. Add the garlic and potatoes and sauté for 5 minutes. Add the broth, soy sauce, paprika, thyme, oregano, onion powder, garlic powder, kosher salt, and black pepper. Bring to a high simmer and cook until the potatoes are tender, about 10 minutes, stirring occasionally.

While the soup simmers, if using fresh corn, cut the corn from the cob. Thinly slice the green onion tops (dark green portions only) and chard.

Drain the cashews. Using a 2-cup glass measuring cup with spout, carefully scoop out about 4 cups of the hot soup and place it in a blender, then add the drained cashews. Blend on high for about 1 minute until smooth and creamy.

Return the mixture to the soup pot, then stir in the corn and simmer for another minute or two until the corn is tender. Taste and add a few additional pinches of salt if desired. Serve warm, garnished with sliced green onions and chard.

Notes
Serve with Kale Caesar Salad with Paprika Croutons (page 89) or Corn Muffins with Green Onions (page 120).

GF* For gluten-free, make sure the soy sauce is gluten-free.

Eggplant Parmesan is a classic Italian dish that Alex and I are quite fond of, but we find the richness is a bit too much for everyday eating. Here's a remix we created to turn it on its head. There's no frying or breading the eggplant and no mountain of gooey cheese. Instead, the eggplant is mixed with white beans, tomatoes, and Italian spices, then baked with basil breadcrumbs and just enough cheese until the kitchen smells divine. It's a cozy casserole that's fitting for a dinner party, since it makes a substantial amount of servings with relatively simple prep. Leftovers also save well for meals throughout the week.

Eggplant Parmesan Casserole

GF* | *Serves 6 TO 8*

Preheat the oven to 425°F.

Prepare the vegetables: Cut the eggplant into ½-inch rings, then into small, bite-sized chunks. Drain the tomatoes. Drain the beans (no need to rinse). In a 13 x 9-inch baking dish, mix together the eggplant, tomatoes, beans, oregano, garlic powder, red pepper flakes, 1½ teaspoons kosher salt, and several grinds of black pepper.

Start the baking: Slide the baking dish into the oven, then place the bread slices on the oven grates next to the pan. After the bread is lightly browned and toasted, about 8 minutes, remove the bread and continue baking the casserole another 17 minutes (for 25 minutes total).

Make the breadcrumbs: Meanwhile, tear the toasted bread into pieces and place them in the bowl of a food processor; process with the basil for a few seconds until reduced to fine crumbles. Add the olive oil, balsamic vinegar, and ¼ teaspoon kosher salt and pulse several times to fully combine.

Finish the baking: After the casserole has baked 25 minutes total (above), remove it from the oven and sprinkle evenly with the mozzarella cheese, then the Parmesan cheese. Top with an even layer of breadcrumbs. Bake for 10 minutes more. Remove from the oven and cool at least 5 minutes before serving.

Notes
Storage: Leftovers can be stored refrigerated for 2 to 3 days; it also freezes well.

GF* For gluten-free, use gluten-free bread.

1 medium eggplant (about 1 pound)
1 28-ounce can diced tomatoes
2 15-ounce cans cannellini beans
1 tablespoon dried oregano
1 teaspoon garlic powder
1 teaspoon red pepper flakes
1¾ teaspoons kosher salt, divided
    Freshly ground black pepper
3 large, thick slices artisan bread (or 6 small slices)
1 cup basil leaves, loosely packed
2 tablespoons extra-virgin olive oil
1 tablespoon balsamic vinegar
1 cup mozzarella cheese
½ cup Parmesan cheese

Loaded Sweet Potato Wedges

with Black Beans

Loaded sweet potatoes were our entry into real food cooking. Something about the contrast of Mexican flavors with the natural sweetness of the potato intrigued us, and we started making it on repeat in our tiny galley kitchen. Since then, we've learned a few things: slicing sweet potatoes into wedges instead of baking them whole cuts the baking time nearly in half. And simmering black beans with a bit of green onion, cilantro, garlic, and smoky chipotle powder brings forth big flavor in a matter of minutes. If time allows, use our recipe for homemade salsa (page 49). These Simplest Black Beans are also used in our burrito bowl (page 187).

GF | V | *Serves 4*

FOR THE SWEET POTATOES

- 4 large sweet potatoes (about 3 pounds)
- 2 tablespoons extra-virgin olive oil
- ½ teaspoon kosher salt

FOR THE SIMPLEST BLACK BEANS

- 4 green onions
- 4 medium garlic cloves
- 1 handful cilantro
- 2 15-ounce cans black beans
- ¼ cup extra-virgin olive oil
- ¼ teaspoon chipotle powder (or substitute ½ teaspoon cumin plus ⅛ teaspoon cayenne)
- ¾ teaspoon kosher salt, plus more to taste

FOR SERVING

- 1 lime
- 2 cups salsa, Roasted Poblano Salsa (page 49) or Peach Salsa Fresca (page 50)
- 1 handful cilantro

  Creamy Cashew Sauce, Mexican or Green variations (page 142) (optional)

Preheat the oven to 450°F.

Roast the potatoes: Cut each sweet potato in half, then in half again to make 4 wedges. Line a baking sheet with parchment paper or a silicone mat, then place the wedges on top. Drizzle with the olive oil and rub the potatoes with your hands to fully coat, then sprinkle with the kosher salt. Bake until tender and slightly browned, about 35 minutes.

Make the black beans: Thinly slice the green onions; reserve the white and light green portions for a garnish and use the dark green top portions for the beans. Smash and peel the garlic. Roughly chop the cilantro. Drain both cans of black beans and reserve ½ cup of the can liquid (no need to rinse).

In a large skillet, heat the olive oil over medium heat. Add the sliced dark green onion tops and whole garlic cloves and sauté for 2 to 3 minutes, until the garlic is golden. Add the beans and stir, taking care to avoid any spitting liquid. Then stir in the reserved can liquid, cilantro, chipotle powder, and kosher salt. Simmer over medium-low heat for about 10 to 12 minutes, stirring occasionally, until most of the liquid has cooked out and the beans are thickened and saucy. Remove and discard the garlic. Taste and add a few additional pinches of salt if desired.

To serve, slice the lime into wedges. Place the potato wedges on a plate. Top with the black beans, salsa, sliced green onions, torn cilantro leaves, and a few squeezes of lime juice. If desired, add a dollop of Creamy Cashew Sauce.

Notes

Make ahead/storage: If made in advance and refrigerated, sweet potatoes can be reheated in a 400°F oven for 10 minutes.

Making a good burrito bowl isn't rocket science, but it's also not as easy as dumping canned black beans and salsa over rice. For our house recipe, our Simplest Black Beans method simmers the beans with a bit of the can liquid, green onion, cilantro, garlic, and smoky chipotle powder. Our other secret is dousing everything with cumin lime crema, a savory sauce made with tahini. Burrito bowls scale well for feeding a crowd, and their self-serve nature makes them sure to please all types of eaters.

Burrito Bowl

with Cumin Lime Crema

GF | **V** | *Serves* **4**

Make the black beans: See the black bean recipe in Loaded Sweet Potato Wedges with Black Beans (page 184).

Make the rice: Prepare the rice (page 136). When cooked, stir in the chili powder, olive oil, and kosher salt.

Make the cumin lime crema: Peel and finely mince the garlic. Juice the limes. In a small bowl, stir together the garlic, lime juice, tahini, hot sauce, cumin, olive oil, and kosher salt. Add 1 to 2 tablespoons water if necessary to achieve a creamy consistency.

Prepare the fresh ingredients: Slice the tomatoes in half. Chop the avocado. Cut the corn off of the cob or warm frozen corn to room temperature.

To serve, place the rice in a bowl. Top with the black beans, tomatoes, avocado, corn, reserved green onions from the black bean recipe, and torn cilantro leaves, then drizzle with cumin lime crema.

Notes
*For sour cream–based crema: Stir together 2 tablespoons lime juice, ½ cup sour cream, 1 tablespoon hot sauce, ½ teaspoon cumin, and ¼ teaspoon kosher salt.

For cashew crema: Make the Green or Mexican Creamy Cashew Sauce on page 142.

FOR THE BEANS AND RICE
Simplest Black Beans (page 184)
- 2 cups uncooked brown or white rice
- 2 teaspoons chili powder
- 1 tablespoon extra-virgin olive oil
- ¼ teaspoon kosher salt

FOR THE CUMIN LIME CREMA
- 1 small garlic clove
- ¼ cup lime juice (2 limes)
- 3 tablespoons tahini*
- 1 tablespoon Mexican hot sauce (we like Cholula)
- ½ teaspoon ground cumin
- 1 tablespoon extra-virgin olive oil
- ¼ teaspoon kosher salt

FOR SERVING
- 1 pint cherry tomatoes
- 1 avocado
- 1 cup corn kernels, fresh or frozen
- 1 handful cilantro

Red Lentil Coconut Curry

with Cilantro Chutney

This recipe is one of the most beloved in this book: the gleaming emerald cilantro chutney mixes tangy and sweet in a sumptuous way that our friends and family can't get enough of. A fusion of Indian and Thai-style curries, the lentils are covered in a sauce of ginger, coconut milk, and red curry paste, an aromatic blend of spices available in the ethnic section of most groceries. Piled atop rice with the famous chutney, they're silky and glamorous in a way most lentils only dream of. Serve with a green salad or with Homemade Whole Wheat Naan (page 122).

GF | **V** | *Serves* **4 TO 6**

FOR THE CURRY

- 2 **cups uncooked brown basmati rice**
- 1 **medium yellow onion**
- 3 **medium garlic cloves**
- 1 **3-inch nub fresh ginger**
- 2 **tablespoons extra-virgin olive oil**
- 1 **cup red lentils**
- 1 **cup canned crushed tomatoes**
- 1 **cup plus 2 tablespoons full-fat coconut milk, divided**
- ¼ **cup red curry paste***
- 2 **tablespoons tomato paste**
- 1 **teaspoon kosher salt**
- 4-5 **cups baby spinach leaves, packed (chopped if leaves are large)**

FOR THE CHUTNEY

- ¼ **cup diced yellow onion (reserved from above)**
- 2 **cups packed cilantro leaves and tender stems**
- ¼ **cup chopped golden raisins**
- 2 **tablespoons white wine vinegar**
- 2 **tablespoons extra-virgin olive oil**
- ½ **teaspoon kosher salt**

Make the brown rice (page 136).

Make the curry: Peel and dice the onion. Reserve ¼ cup for the chutney and set aside; use the remaining portion for the curry. Peel and mince the garlic. Peel and mince the ginger and measure out 2 tablespoons. In a large skillet, heat the olive oil over medium-high heat, then add the onion and sauté until translucent, about 5 minutes. Add the garlic and ginger and sauté for 1 minute.

Add the lentils, tomatoes, 1 cup coconut milk, 2 cups water, red curry paste, tomato paste, and kosher salt. Bring to a simmer and cook very gently, just barely bubbling, for 10 to 15 minutes until the lentils are soft (if not, cook a few minutes more until tender). Stir in the spinach along with 2 tablespoons coconut milk and cook until the leaves wilt. Taste and add additional kosher salt or coconut milk to taste.

Make the chutney: Meanwhile, make the chutney using an immersion blender or standard blender to blend the reserved ¼ cup diced onion, cilantro, golden raisins, white wine vinegar, olive oil, kosher salt, and ¼ cup water. Blend into a thick, smooth sauce.

To serve, spoon the lentils over rice and top with a dollop of chutney.

Notes

*If your brand of red curry paste is very spicy, add it in gradually to taste. Our preferred brand adds flavor without excessive heat, but make sure to taste test before adding the entire amount.

Roasted Cauliflower & Black Bean Tacos

with Chipotle Aïoli

If you're in the mood for fancy tacos, here's your recipe: turmeric-roasted cauliflower and refried black beans smothered in a savory, chipotle aïoli. Inspired by a meal I had in Austin, Texas, the aïoli whisks together in a minute; it's essentially a homemade mayonnaise. Topped with cilantro, lime, pepitas, and radishes, the contrast of flavors and textures is divine. The finishing touch is another trick I learned in Texas from our friend Jeanine Donofrio, author of *The Love and Lemons Cookbook*: blackening the tortillas over an open flame on the stovetop softens them and adds a charred flavor. If you're looking for quick weeknight tacos, try our Quick Fix Pinto Bean Tacos instead (page 156).

GF | V* | *Serves* **4 TO 6**

FOR THE CAULIFLOWER
Double recipe Turmeric Roasted Cauliflower (page 114)

FOR THE BEANS
- 1 small white onion
- 2 15-ounce cans black beans
- 1 tablespoon unsalted butter
- 2 tablespoons extra-virgin olive oil
- ½ teaspoon kosher salt
- ½ teaspoon chili powder
- ¼ teaspoon freshly ground black pepper

FOR THE CHIPOTLE AÏOLI*
- 1 egg yolk
- ½ teaspoon Dijon mustard
- ⅓ cup extra-virgin olive oil
- 1 small garlic clove
- ¼ teaspoon kosher salt
- 1 tablespoon adobo sauce (from 1 can chipotle peppers in adobo sauce)**

FOR THE TACOS
- 8 tortillas
- 4 radishes
- 1 large handful cilantro
- 1 lime
- ¼ cup roasted salted pepitas

Make the cauliflower: Make a double recipe following the instructions on page 114.

Make the refried beans: Peel and halve the onion, then thinly slice it into half-moon shapes. Drain the beans, reserving ½ cup of the can liquid.

In a medium saucepan, heat the butter and olive oil over medium heat. Add the onion and sauté until translucent, 3 to 4 minutes. Add the beans, reserved can liquid, kosher salt, chili powder, and black pepper. Turn the heat to medium low and cook for 10 to 15 minutes, stirring often and smashing the beans toward the end of the cook time, until most of the liquid has cooked out and the texture is mashed and thick. Scrape the bottom and sides of the pan as necessary. Taste and season with additional salt as desired.

Make the chipotle aïoli: Place a medium-sized, flat-bottomed bowl on top of a folded dish towel to keep it secure while whisking. The size of the bowl is important, as it must be large enough to allow for whisking vigorously. Add the egg yolk and mustard to the bowl and whisk until thick and creamy. Pour the olive oil into a liquid measuring cup. Starting one drop at a time, slowly add the olive oil into the egg mixture, whisking constantly. Allow the olive oil to become completely incorporated before continuing to add more olive oil; the drizzling can become gradually faster as you go. Whisk until all of the oil is fully incorporated and the aïoli is thickened. Peel and mince the garlic clove. Sprinkle it with a very small pinch of salt, then holding the blunt edge of the knife, scrape the sharp edge of the blade over the minced garlic, holding the knife at an angle and mashing the garlic into a paste. Stir the garlic paste, kosher salt, and adobo sauce into the aïoli. (Store the leftover aïoli in an airtight container in the refrigerator for several weeks; bring to room temperature before serving.)

Char the tortillas: Turn on a gas burner to medium heat and place the tortilla directly on the grate. After about 15 seconds when the edges are lightly charred, use tongs to flip the tortilla and heat on the opposite side until lightly charred. Repeat for all tortillas, taking care that they do not catch fire.

Prepare the garnishes: Thinly slice the radishes. Slice the lime into wedges.

To serve, place a layer of refried black beans in a tortilla, then top with roasted cauliflower. Add pepitas, torn cilantro leaves, a squeeze of lime, radishes, and a drizzle of chipotle aïoli.

Notes
Make ahead/storage: Roast the cauliflower, make the black beans, and make the aïoli, then store them refrigerated. The day of serving, warm the cauliflower in a 400°F oven for about 10 minutes, reheat the black beans in a pan on the stovetop, and bring the aïoli to room temperature.

For an alternative without raw egg: Mix ½ cup mayonnaise with 1 small garlic clove (ground to a paste as described), ½ teaspoon Dijon mustard, ¼ teaspoon kosher salt, and 1 tablespoon adobo sauce. Add 1 teaspoon or so of water to bring the sauce to a consistency that can be drizzled.

****Use 1 tablespoon adobo sauce from the can; the peppers and remaining sauce can be reserved (or frozen) for future use.

V* For vegan, use Cumin Lime Crema (page 187).

Grilled Portobello Fajitas

There's nothing quite like the smoky smell of firing up a charcoal grill on a summer evening. At our house, you're just as likely to find vegetables on the grill as meat or fish. Dressed up as a fajita, these mushrooms can hold their own against steak. Nestled with grilled peppers and onions in a soft corn tortilla, their juicy, meaty texture is hard to resist, even for self-proclaimed mushroom haters. We serve them with grilled pinto beans for additional protein, which can be warmed alongside the vegetables in a separate foil packet.

GF | **V*** | *Serves* **4 TO 6**

FOR THE FAJITAS

- 4 medium portobello mushrooms (about 12 ounces)
- 1 medium red onion
- 1 red bell pepper
- 1 orange bell pepper
- 1 poblano pepper
- 3 medium garlic cloves
- ¼ cup lime juice (2 limes)
- 1 tablespoon cumin
- 1 tablespoon adobo sauce (from 1 can chipotle peppers in adobo sauce)*
- 2 teaspoons kosher salt
- ¼ cup extra-virgin olive oil

FOR THE PINTO BEANS

- 1 15-ounce can pinto beans
- 1 small or ½ medium white onion
- ½ teaspoon kosher salt
- 1 tablespoon extra-virgin olive oil
- 12 corn tortillas
- Sour cream, for serving

Heat a grill to medium high.

Prepare the vegetables: Brush any dirt from the mushrooms, remove the stems, and slice them into long thin strips. Peel and thinly slice the red onion. Remove pith and seeds from the bell peppers and poblano pepper and thinly slice. Place the mushrooms, onion, and peppers together in a large bowl.

Peel and mince the garlic. Juice the limes. In a small bowl, whisk together the garlic, lime juice, cumin, adobo sauce, kosher salt, and olive oil. Pour the mixture into the bowl of vegetables and mix with your hands to ensure all are thoroughly coated.

Prepare the beans: Drain the beans (no need to rinse). Peel and thinly slice the white onion. Prepare a piece of aluminum foil 16 inches long; place the beans and onion on the foil and mix with the kosher salt and olive oil. Fold up the sides of the foil and seal it tightly into a packet.

Grill the vegetables and beans: Fold a large piece of aluminum foil in half and prick several holes in it with a fork, then fold up a 1-inch rim around the edge to make a makeshift tray. Place the foil tray on the hot grill and pile the vegetables on top, noting that the vegetables cook down significantly as they grill so they'll form a large mound at first. Grill the vegetables for 15 to 20 minutes, stirring occasionally, until tender and slightly charred. While the vegetables cook, place the bean packet on the grill and grill away from the main heat source until the vegetables are done.

To serve, place the vegetables and beans in a warmed tortilla, and top with a dollop of sour cream.

V* For vegan, omit the sour cream.

Veggie Supreme Paella

GF | V | *Serves 6*

My Spanish host Marta and her mother María Rosa introduced me to this traditional dish during my time studying in Madrid. Paella quickly stole my heart. Now, Alex and I love to make paella for occasions like birthdays or Valentine's Day, but this version is even simple enough for a weeknight. A key ingredient is *pimentón*—Spanish smoked paprika—which adds smokiness and a rosy color to the dish. Pricey and hard to find, saffron is also traditionally used along with the *pimentón*, but we've found that turmeric works for everyday cooking. Although a large skillet is all you need for this one-pot meal, you also can use the recipe as an excuse to buy a traditional two-handled paella pan (they're easy to find online and can also be used on a grill and over an open fire). Serve the paella with a green salad, marinated olives (page 69), and a Spanish red wine.

1 small yellow onion
4 medium garlic cloves
1 small head or ½ large cauliflower
8 ounces shiitake mushrooms
1 handful green beans (about 3 ounces)
1 large roasted red pepper (from a jar)
1 15-ounce can chickpeas
3 tablespoons extra-virgin olive oil
1 15-ounce can diced fire-roasted tomatoes
1½ cups dry white arborio rice
1½ tablespoons smoked paprika (pimentón)
½ teaspoon turmeric or pinch saffron
1½ teaspoons kosher salt
3½ cups vegetable broth

Peel and dice the onion. Peel and mince the garlic. Chop the cauliflower into florets. Brush any dirt from the mushrooms, remove the tough stems, and slice the tops. Remove the ends of the green beans. Thinly slice the red pepper. Drain and rinse the chickpeas.

In a large skillet (at least 12 inches) or paella pan, drizzle a bit of olive oil and heat it over medium heat. Add the green beans and sauté for 2 to 3 minutes until bright green, slightly tender and charred in parts; remove from the pan and set aside. Add 3 tablespoons olive oil to the hot pan, and sauté the onion until just translucent, about 4 minutes. Add the garlic, cauliflower, and mushrooms, and sauté for about 1 minute until the garlic is fragrant. Add the tomatoes with their liquid, and cook until all liquid is reduced, about 6 to 7 minutes. Stir in the rice, smoked paprika, turmeric (or saffron), and kosher salt. Stirring constantly, cook for about 1 minute until the rice is well coated. Add the broth and chickpeas and stir to combine. Arrange the green beans on top, slightly pressing them into the rice, then sprinkle the red pepper strips over the top. Bring to a simmer.

Allow the liquid to slowly absorb at a medium simmer, gently bubbling; do not stir. Avoiding stirring allows a bit of crusty rice on the bottom and edges of the pan, while the remainder of the rice stays tender. Cook until the rice is al dente and all bubbling has stopped, about 25 to 30 minutes depending on the pan. Take care that the simmer is gentle; if the heat is too high, the rice on the bottom may burn. (If you're using a paella pan, place it across two stovetop burners and rotate it occasionally to make sure all sides cook evenly.) When the rice is done, remove from the heat and serve immediately.

Moroccan Sweet Potato Stew *with Quinoa*

This cozy stew is loaded with North African spices: cumin, coriander, turmeric, cinnamon, and ginger—which are balanced with the sweetness of apricots and brightened with lemon. While the ingredient list is deceptively long, it's actually quite easy to put together—and you can clean the kitchen while it simmers. We've served it for just the two of us, as a Friday-night dinner for guests, and even brought it to new parents. Serve it over quinoa, garnished with cilantro and a bit of tangy yogurt.

GF | **V*** | *Serves 4 TO 6*

- 2 cups uncooked quinoa
- 1 large yellow onion
- 3 medium garlic cloves
- 1½ pounds sweet potatoes (about 2 medium size)
- ⅓ cup chopped dried apricots
- 1 15-ounce can chickpeas
- 2 teaspoons ground cumin
- 2 teaspoons ground coriander
- 1 teaspoon turmeric
- 1 teaspoon cinnamon
- 1 teaspoon dried ground ginger
- ¼ teaspoon red pepper flakes
- 2 tablespoons extra-virgin olive oil
- 1¼ teaspoons kosher salt, divided
- Freshly ground black pepper
- 1 15-ounce can diced tomatoes
- 1 quart (4 cups) vegetable broth
- 6 cups baby spinach leaves, loosely packed (chopped if leaves are large)
- 3–4 tablespoons lemon juice (1 large lemon)
- 1 handful cilantro, for garnish
- Greek yogurt or crème fraîche (page 139), for serving

Make the quinoa (page 134).

Peel and dice the onion. Peel and mince the garlic. Chop the sweet potatoes into ½-inch pieces, leaving the skin on. Roughly chop the apricots. Drain and rinse the chickpeas. Combine the cumin, coriander, turmeric, cinnamon, ginger, and red pepper flakes in a small bowl.

In a large pot or Dutch oven, heat 2 tablespoons olive oil over medium-high heat. Sauté the onion for about 5 minutes, until translucent. Add the garlic and sauté until fragrant, about 30 seconds. Stir in the spices, 1 teaspoon kosher salt, and several grinds of black pepper. Stir about 30 seconds, then add the sweet potatoes, apricots, chickpeas, tomatoes, and vegetable broth.

Bring to a boil, then simmer for 20 to 25 minutes until the potatoes are tender and beginning to break down and the liquid is reduced. Stir in the spinach and simmer until wilted, about 2 minutes. Remove from the heat and allow to cool slightly.

Immediately prior to serving, stir in the lemon juice and ¼ teaspoon kosher salt. Serve with quinoa, garnished with torn cilantro leaves and a dollop of Greek yogurt.

V* For vegan, omit the Greek yogurt or substitute Creamy Cashew Sauce (page 142).

White Cheddar Leek & Greens Millet Bake

Alex's stepfather is as meat-and-potatoes as they come, and before this casserole, he'd never seen leeks, chard, or millet used in the kitchen. But his reaction to the first bite was just what we'd hoped: "Wow." Millet is a lesser-known whole grain that's actually a seed and naturally gluten-free like its trendier cousin quinoa. Here we've combined it with sautéed leeks and rainbow chard and a creamy white cheddar thyme sauce. Alex and I like to make up a big pan and live off leftovers for nights when time doesn't allow for cooking. The concept is based on a broccoli cheddar millet bake from our website; when a reader commented that her teenage sons raved about it, we knew we had to include a version here.

GF | *Serves* **6 TO 8**

- 1½ **cups millet**
- 1½ **teaspoons kosher salt, divided**
- 2 **large leeks**
- 2 **bunches rainbow chard or any leafy green (about 1 pound)**
- 3 **medium garlic cloves**
- 2 **tablespoons extra-virgin olive oil**
  Freshly ground black pepper
- 8 **ounces sharp white Cheddar cheese**
- 1 **tablespoon unsalted butter**
- 1 **cup 2% milk**
- 1 **scant teaspoon dried thyme**

Preheat the oven to 425°F.

Make the millet: Pour the millet into a dry saucepan and toast for 2 to 3 minutes over medium heat, stirring frequently. Reduce the heat and carefully add 3 cups water. Bring to a boil, then reduce the heat to very low. Cover the pot and simmer where the water is just bubbling for about 17 minutes, until the water has been completely absorbed (check by pulling back the millet with a fork). Remove from the heat, then cover the pot and allow the millet to steam until baking. Uncover and stir in a mounded ¼ teaspoon kosher salt.

Sauté the leeks and chard: Chop off the dark green stems of the leeks and the tough roots, then slice them in half lengthwise. Place each leek half cut-side down and thinly slice it, resulting in half-moon shapes. Rinse the slices thoroughly in a colander to remove any dirt, and shake off the remaining water.

Destem the chard by holding the leaf at the lowest part of the stem and pulling back to tear the leaf away from the stem, then roughly chop the leaves. Peel and mince the garlic and set it aside.

In a large skillet over medium-high heat, heat the olive oil. Add the leeks and sauté about 3 minutes, until tender but before browning. Add the chard and sauté for 1 to 2 minutes until wilted. Stir in ¼ teaspoon kosher salt and several grinds of black pepper, then remove the mixture to a bowl and wipe out the skillet.

Make the sauce: Shred the cheese. In the same skillet, heat the butter over medium-low heat. Add the garlic and sauté for 1 minute. Add the milk, thyme, and 1 teaspoon kosher salt and bring to a simmer. Stir in 1½ cups shredded cheese and stir until the cheese melts and the sauce thickens slightly (increase the heat slightly if the cheese does not melt at first, but take care not to overheat).

Bake: Evenly spread the millet into a 13 x 9-inch baking dish. Spread the sautéed leeks and greens over the top, and pour on the sauce. Stir the ingredients together roughly with a fork to combine the millet with the sauce and cheese. Sprinkle the remaining shredded cheese over the top. Bake for 15 minutes until the cheese is melted. Allow to cool for a few minutes, then serve warm.

Notes

Storage: Leftovers can be stored refrigerated for 2 to 3 days; it also freezes well.

Turmeric Rice Bowls

with Lemon Tahini Drizzle

With its bright yellow rice, fuchsia carrot ribbons, and gleaming glazed tempeh, we've served this bowl to impress eaters of all kinds, not just hipster vegetarian types. Tempeh is one of the only "meat substitutes" that we eat regularly—the pressed soybeans give it a firm texture and a nutty taste that is entirely different from its cousin tofu. Here it's sliced and marinated in a soy-maple glaze, nestled with quick-sautéed broccoli and kale, and drizzled with a tangy lemon tahini dressing. The components are all simple, but for a weeknight meal you may want to prepare a few of them in advance. Tempeh, turmeric, and tahini are available at most supermarkets and absolutely worth the hunt.

GF | V | *Serves 4*

FOR THE RICE

- 1½ cups long grain brown rice
- 2 teaspoons turmeric
- ½ teaspoon kosher salt

FOR THE LEMON TAHINI DRIZZLE*

- ¼ cup tahini
- 3 tablespoons fresh lemon juice (1 large lemon)
- 1 tablespoon extra-virgin olive oil
- ⅛ teaspoon garlic powder
- ¼ teaspoon kosher salt

FOR THE VEGETABLES

- 2 medium garlic cloves
- 2 large bunches broccoli
- 1 large bunch Tuscan or Lacinato kale (about 12 ounces)
- 2 tablespoons extra-virgin olive oil
- 2 tablespoons soy sauce or tamari
- ¼ teaspoon kosher salt

FOR THE TEMPEH

- 2 medium garlic cloves
- 3 tablespoons extra-virgin olive oil, divided
- 2 tablespoons soy sauce or tamari
- 1 tablespoon white wine vinegar
- 1 tablespoon pure maple syrup
- 8 ounces tempeh

Make the rice: Boil the rice using the method on page 136, adding the turmeric in with the rice. After steaming, add the kosher salt. Note that as it boils, extra turmeric will build up around the pot rim; it easily washes off after cooking.

Make the tahini drizzle: In a small bowl, combine the tahini, lemon juice, olive oil, garlic powder, kosher salt, and 2 tablespoons water. Stir vigorously to combine; add another tablespoon or so of water if necessary to obtain a creamy sauce that is able to drizzle. The sauce is very forgiving; if it becomes too loose, mix in a bit more tahini. (If making in advance, store the sauce refrigerated and bring to room temperature prior to serving.)

Sauté the vegetables: Peel the garlic and leave it whole. Chop the broccoli into florets. Destem the kale by holding the leaf at the lowest part of the stem and pulling back to tear the leaf away from the stem, then chop the leaves into roughly bite-sized pieces. In a large skillet, heat the olive oil with the whole garlic cloves until the garlic starts to sizzle. Add the broccoli and sauté for 3 minutes. Add the kale and ¼ cup water and sauté for 1 to 2 minutes, stirring, until the leaves are bright green and wilted. Add the soy sauce and sprinkle with the kosher salt, then sauté another 1 to 2 minutes. Remove the vegetables from the skillet to a bowl and cover to keep warm until serving. Wipe out the skillet and discard the garlic cloves.

Cook the tempeh: Peel and finely mince the garlic. Place the garlic in a small bowl with 1 tablespoon olive oil, soy sauce, white wine vinegar, and maple syrup. Slice the tempeh into ¼-inch-thick rectangular strips. In the same skillet, heat 2 tablespoons olive oil over medium heat. Add the tempeh slices (large rectangular side down) in a single layer and cook on one side until browned, about 3 to 5 minutes, then flip and cook another 3 to 5 minutes until

browned on the other side. Reduce the heat to medium low and pour in the soy-maple mixture. Cook another 5 to 6 minutes until the tempeh is evenly browned and the liquid is mostly reduced, shaking the pan occasionally and flipping the tempeh one more time before the liquid is completely reduced. When browned, remove the tempeh from the heat into a bowl.

Prepare the garnishes: Using a vegetable peeler, peel the carrots into long ribbons. Thinly slice the green onions on the bias.

To serve, place the rice in bowls, then top with the broccoli, kale, tempeh, carrot ribbons, and green onions. Drizzle with lemon tahini dressing and serve.

Notes
*For a cashew drizzle: Swap out the lemon tahini drizzle for the Creamy Cashew Sauce on page 142.

Make ahead: Make the rice, tahini drizzle, and broccoli and kale in advance. The day of serving, reheat the rice using the instructions on page 136, and cook the tempeh.

FOR THE GARNISHES
- 4 **rainbow carrots**
- 2 **green onions**

"Eating with the fullest pleasure...
is perhaps the profoundest enactment
of our connection with the world."

—WENDELL BERRY, "THE PLEASURES OF EATING"

Respect the ingredients.

Slowing down and cooking more connects us not just to the people around the table but to the big picture behind the ingredients we use. You can't taste a locally grown strawberry at its peak of juicy summer sweetness without being grateful for the dark soil that made it flourish. The perfect simplicity of ruby heirloom tomatoes and cool cucumber in a Greek salad inspires a respect for the land where they grow.

As eaters, we start to understand our place in the process: to appreciate the planting, growing, and harvesting, to value the Earth and its vast array of flavors, and to care deeply for both the land and the farmers who lovingly sacrifice to make it happen. Instead of mere consumers, we are participants in the cycle of seed to table.

Eating beautiful, quality ingredients is not just for the gourmet or the hipster or the eco-nerd. It's also not only for the rich: a pot of boiled beans and a tiny basil plant are available to all. Respecting the Earth and her seasons, valuing the local farmer and the ethical olive oil producer, appreciating quality over quantity—this is something all eaters can embrace.

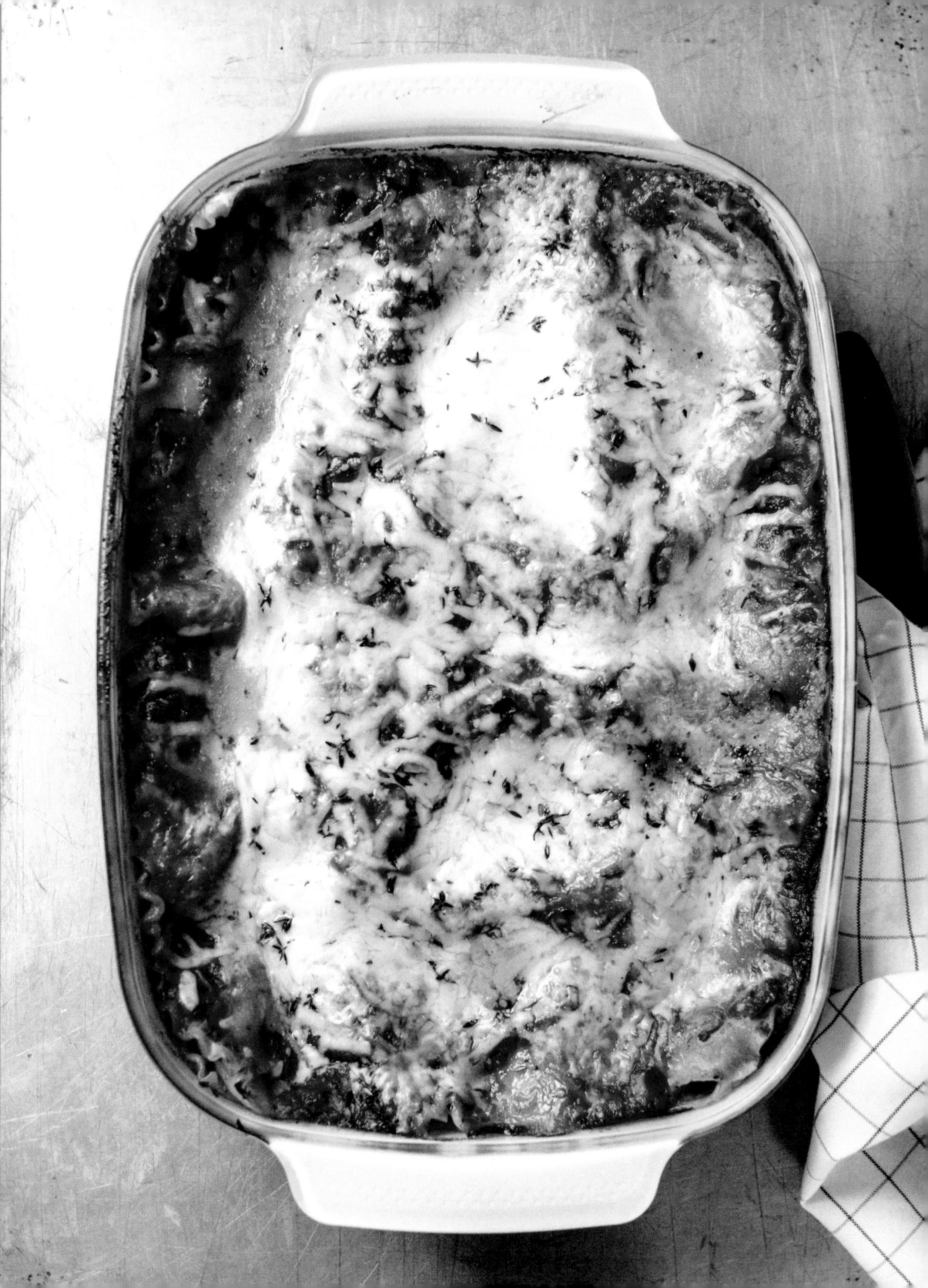

Mains
Special Occasions

Roasted Acorn Squash

with Brown Rice Sausage & Kale

A common way to serve roasted squash is stuffed with sausage and rice. On a whim, we tried creating a meatless version by mixing sausage spices with brown rice and walnuts—and surprisingly, it worked! The trick is fennel seeds, which are traditionally used in Italian sausage; you may find your brain associates their flavor with sausage pizza. A few more savory spices, aromatics, and kale round out the filling, and it makes for a particularly showy vegetarian entrée for occasions like Sunday dinners or Thanksgiving.

GF | **V*** | *Serves 8*

- 1 cup medium or short grain brown rice
- 2 cups vegetable broth
- 2 tablespoons olive oil, divided, plus more for drizzling
- 4 large acorn squash (about 1½ pounds each)
- 2 large carrots
- 2 stalks celery
- 1 small yellow onion
- 1 large shallot (or 2 small)
- ½ bunch Tuscan or Lacinato kale (about 4 ounces)
- ⅔ cup chopped walnuts
- 2 tablespoons unsalted butter
- 1½ teaspoons fennel seeds
- 1 teaspoon dried ground sage
- 1 teaspoon garlic powder
- 1 teaspoon onion powder
- 1 teaspoon paprika
- ¼ teaspoon crushed red pepper flakes
- ¾ teaspoon kosher salt, plus more for sprinkling
- ¼ teaspoon ground black pepper, plus more for sprinkling

Preheat the oven to 450°F.

Make the rice: In a medium saucepan, bring the rice, vegetable broth, and 1 tablespoon olive oil to a boil. Cover and simmer gently until the broth is entirely absorbed, about 35 minutes (timing may vary depending on brand; check by pulling back the rice with a fork). Remove from the heat and allow to steam, covered, for about 10 minutes or until used in the recipe.

Roast the squash: Chop each squash into quarters and use a spoon to scrape out the seeds. Line a baking sheet with parchment paper or a silicone mat, and place the squash onto the sheet. Drizzle the cut sides with olive oil, then sprinkle a few pinches kosher salt and several grinds of black pepper. Place cut-side down on the sheet and roast until tender, about 35 to 40 minutes.

Assemble the filling: Peel the carrots. Finely chop the carrot and celery. Peel and mince the onion and the shallot. Destem the kale by holding the leaf at the lowest part of the stem and pulling back to tear the leaf away from the stem, then finely chop the leaves (about 2 cups). Chop the walnuts.

In a large skillet over medium-high heat, melt the butter and 1 tablespoon olive oil. Add the carrot, celery, onion, shallot, and fennel seeds and sauté until tender and fragrant, about 5 minutes. Add the kale and sauté until tender, another 2 minutes. Stir in the rice, walnuts, sage, garlic powder, onion powder, paprika, red pepper flakes, kosher salt, and black pepper. Mix to fully combine and heat the filling, then remove from the heat.

Serve the squash topped with a few spoonfuls of filling, allowing it to spill over the sides.

Notes

Make ahead: Make the filling and squash in advance. On the day of serving, reheat the filling in a skillet with a drizzle of additional olive oil. Warm the squash in a 400°F oven for 10 minutes.

V* For vegan, substitute 2 tablespoons olive oil for the butter.

Ricotta Gnocchi alla Vodka

This is our beloved date night in—homemade pasta. Rolling out sheets of noodles can be time consuming, so we prefer making gnocchi, fresh pillowy dumplings drenched in a savory sauce. Alex and I first fell in love with gnocchi on the cobblestone streets in Rome somewhere near the glow of the Pantheon, and we've perfected a pretty simple method for making them at home. Instead of the traditional potato version, these gnocchi are made with ricotta cheese, which gets them on the table in about 1 hour. They're topped with our simplest vodka sauce, where the vodka leaves behind a fruity complexity once the alcohol is cooked out, and Greek yogurt makes the sauce creamy without the over-the-top richness of traditional heavy cream. While homemade pasta is a project, it makes the best memories, like laughing over a bottle of wine with my husband and sister on a snowy December evening, or rolling out long strands on a February double-date with friends.

Serves 4

FOR THE VODKA SAUCE

- ¾ cup minced shallots (2 large)
- 2 medium garlic cloves
- 2 tablespoons unsalted butter
- 1 28-ounce can crushed tomatoes
- ⅓ cup high-quality vodka*
- 1 teaspoon dried oregano
- ⅛ teaspoon nutmeg
- ¼ teaspoon red pepper flakes
- 1 teaspoon kosher salt
  Freshly ground black pepper
- 1 tablespoon extra-virgin olive oil
- ⅓ cup plain whole milk Greek yogurt

FOR THE GNOCCHI

- 1 tablespoon (for the pasta water) plus 1 teaspoon kosher salt, divided
- 2 large eggs
- 16 ounces (2 cups) whole milk ricotta
- ¾ cup grated Parmesan cheese, plus more for serving
- 1 teaspoon dried oregano
- ½ teaspoon ground black pepper
- ½ cup whole wheat flour
- ¾ cup all-purpose flour
- 1 handful fresh basil (optional)

Start the vodka sauce: Peel and mince the shallots. Peel and mince the garlic.

In a large saucepan, warm the butter over medium-low heat. Add the shallots and sauté until translucent, stirring occasionally, about 2 to 3 minutes. Add the garlic and stir until fragrant, about 30 seconds.

Remove the pan from the burner and carefully pour in the tomatoes, then add it back to heat and stir in the vodka, oregano, nutmeg, red pepper flakes, kosher salt, and several grinds of black pepper. Bring to a bubble, then reduce the heat and simmer on low for at least 20 minutes (sauce instructions continue).

Make the gnocchi: Meanwhile, fill a large pot with 6 quarts of water and 1 tablespoon kosher salt and bring it to a boil.

In a large bowl, lightly beat the eggs. Add the ricotta, Parmesan cheese, oregano, black pepper, and 1 teaspoon kosher salt. Mix until well combined. Add the whole wheat flour and all-purpose flour and stir until just combined. Lightly flour a countertop, then turn out the dough and gently knead a few times until a very sticky dough forms; a sticky texture is desired at this point. Divide the dough into 8 equal portions; wash your hands to remove the dough coating.

Have a baking sheet ready. Lightly flour the countertop again. Roll one of the portions into a log about 14 inches long and ½ inch in diameter. Use a butter knife to cut the dough into 1-inch-long

pillows. Place the formed gnocchi on the baking sheet. Reflour the countertop and shape another dough; repeat until all gnocchi are formed.

Boil the gnocchi in four batches, cooking until the gnocchi float for 30 seconds (about 2 to 3 minutes per batch). Remove them with a slotted spoon and place on a plate or baking sheet. Make sure the water remains at a steady boil for the entire cooking time.

Finish the vodka sauce: Return to the vodka sauce. In a small bowl, stir the olive oil into the yogurt, then stir in ⅓ cup of the warm sauce to temper the yogurt and prevent curdling. Scrape the yogurt mixture back into the saucepan and stir to incorporate fully. If desired, you can blend the sauce for a completely smooth texture; we prefer ours chunky.

To serve, mix the gnocchi with the vodka sauce. If desired, top with shredded Parmesan cheese and thinly sliced fresh basil.

Notes
*If you can, try to find vodka from a local distillery.

Vegetarian Lentil Gyros

Gyros are one of our ultimate sandwiches—spiced, juicy lamb strips stuffed in a pita with a creamy yogurt sauce. Naturally, they tasted even better in the warm ocean breeze of the Greek isles. After returning home, Alex had the crazy idea of creating a meatless gyro using lentils. Though it's not as juicy as lamb, this lentil-based version gets pretty close, especially since the heart of gyros are the toppings and sauce. Lentil gyros even have a few improvements over the traditional—they're lighter, nutrient dense, and far cheaper to make. We like to wrap the pita bread in aluminum foil like at a street gyros vendor (and, it makes them easier to eat). For a Greek dinner party, make the gyros and invite friends to bring the following sides: Red Pepper Tabbouleh (page 82), Creamy Artichoke Hummus (page 42), Layered Mediterranean Hummus Platter (page 54), Baked Pita Crisps (page 61), Rosemary Olives with Lemon Zest (page 69), and Classic Greek Salad (page 81).

GF | *Serves* **8**

FOR THE GYROS

- 1¼ cups green lentils
- 8 medium garlic cloves
- 4 3-inch sprigs fresh rosemary
- 8 ounces baby bella (cremini) mushrooms
- 1 tablespoon dried oregano
- 1 tablespoon dried thyme
- 1 teaspoon dried cumin
- 1 teaspoon paprika
- 1 teaspoon coriander
- 1 teaspoon garlic powder
- 1 teaspoon ground black pepper
- 2 tablespoons extra-virgin olive oil
- ½ cup rolled oats
- 1 teaspoon kosher salt
- 2 eggs
- 2 tablespoons salted butter

FOR SERVING

- Yogurt Dill Sauce (page 212)*
- 1 small red onion
- 1 English cucumber
- 1 romaine heart
- 1 tomato
- 8 pita breads or flatbreads

Preheat the oven to 425°F.

Make the gyros: In a saucepan, combine the lentils with 3½ cups water. Bring to a boil, reduce the heat and simmer uncovered until tender, about 20 minutes, then drain.

Meanwhile, peel the garlic and remove the leaves from the rosemary sprigs. Place both in the bowl of a large food processor and process for a few seconds until minced. Brush any dirt from the mushrooms; add them to the bowl and pulse several times until chopped. Mix together the oregano, thyme, cumin, paprika, coriander, garlic powder, and black pepper in a small bowl. In a large skillet over medium heat, heat the olive oil; add the mushroom mixture and sauté for about 4 minutes until tender. Stir in spices and sauté for 1 minute, then remove from the heat. Rinse out the bowl of the food processor.

When the lentils are done, add the lentils, mushroom mixture, oats, and kosher salt to the food processor and pulse a few times until crumbly. Add the eggs and pulse a few times until fully combined but not puréed.

Line a rimmed baking sheet with parchment paper or a silicone mat, and grease the inside of the rim. Spread the lentil mixture about ½ inch thick, filling a little over half of the sheet. Slice the butter into thin pats and evenly space them on top of the lentils. Bake 30 minutes, until browned. Remove the baked lentils from the oven and allow them to rest for 10 minutes. Then slide the parchment out onto a cutting board and carefully slice the lentils into 48 rectangular pieces, each about 3 inches long and ¾ inch wide.

Prepare the toppings: While the gyros bake, make the Yogurt Dill Sauce (page 212). Peel and thinly slice the red onion and rinse it under cold water to mellow the sharp taste. Peel and thinly slice the cucumber. Chop the romaine. Dice the tomato.

Warm the pita bread: Once the oven is turned off after the lentils roast, place the pita breads inside the still warm oven for about 2 minutes until pliable, then place them on a plate under a towel until ready to serve.

To serve, place a few slices of the gyros on the pita bread; top with vegetables and add liberal dollops of Yogurt Dill Sauce to coat the gyros and veggies. Fold the pita around the filling like a taco and wrap the end with aluminum foil. Serve with extra sauce for dolloping.

Notes

Make ahead: Make the gyros in advance and allow them to sit covered at room temperature until serving, then warm them in a 200°F oven prior to eating. Make the yogurt sauce and refrigerate until serving.

Storage: Store leftover gyros in a sealed container in the refrigerator for 2 to 3 days. Or, place the sliced gyros in a sealed plastic bag and freeze for 1 to 2 months. To reheat, place the gyros on a baking sheet, cover with aluminum foil, and bake at 350°F for 7 to 10 minutes.

*For dairy-free, serve with Lemon Tahini Drizzle (page 200) and substitute a light drizzle of olive oil for the butter.

Falafel Burgers

with Yogurt Dill Sauce

GF* | V* | *Makes* **8 BURGERS**

For us, falafel is tied with gyros (page 210) for the award of best sandwich ever—funny enough, they're both Greek in origin. Our first true falafel was not in Greece but Paris, at a busy shop in the winding maze of streets of Le Marais. The crispy-fried chickpea fritters won our hearts, nestled in a doughy pita with messy sauces that ran down our chins and onto our fingers. Since the traditional method of deep-frying falafel can be a hassle at home, this version is a burger that's lightly pan-fried to crisp the outsides, then baked and served with a silky-smooth yogurt dill sauce. If you're short on time, try Chickpea Shawarma Flatbread (page 148) instead for similar flavors in just a few minutes.

FOR THE FALAFEL

- 2 15-ounce cans chickpeas (3 cups cooked)
- ¼ cup sesame seeds
- 6 medium garlic cloves
- 1 medium red onion
- 2 large carrots
- 1 cup packed cilantro leaves and tender stems
- ¾ cup whole wheat flour
- 4 teaspoons cumin
- 4 teaspoons coriander
- ¼ teaspoon cayenne
- 1½ teaspoons kosher salt
- 1 teaspoon freshly ground black pepper
- 2 tablespoons extra-virgin olive oil

FOR THE YOGURT DILL SAUCE

- 2 small garlic cloves
- 2 tablespoons chopped fresh dill
- ¼ cup lemon juice (1 large lemon)
- 2 cups whole milk plain Greek yogurt
- 2 tablespoons extra-virgin olive oil
- ½ teaspoon kosher salt

FOR SERVING

- 1 cucumber
- 1 large tomato
- 8 English muffins

Preheat the oven to 375°F.

Make the burgers: Drain and rinse the chickpeas. Blot them with a paper towel or clean dish towel to remove any extra moisture, then place them in the bowl of a large food processor. Add the sesame seeds and process for a minute or so until a paste-like consistency is formed (if necessary, stop and scrape the sides of the bowl, and process again). Scrape the mixture into a large bowl.

Peel the garlic, red onion, and carrots. Chop the onion and carrot in rough chunks. Add the garlic to the food processor and process until finely chopped. Add the carrot and onion and pulse several times until finely chopped. Add the cilantro to the processor and pulse a few more times until chopped. Scrape the vegetables into the bowl with the chickpeas.

Stir in the flour, cumin, coriander, cayenne, kosher salt, and black pepper. Mix with a spoon or with your hands until fully combined, then form 8 round patties and place them on a baking sheet.

In a large skillet, heat 1 tablespoon olive oil over medium-high heat. Add 4 of the burgers and fry them for 1 to 2 minutes per side, until golden brown. Remove the cooked burgers and place them back on the baking sheet. Wipe out the pan, add an additional drizzle of oil, and fry the remaining 4 burgers, keeping in mind that the pan will be hotter and the cooking time slightly quicker for the second batch.

Once all burgers are browned, place them in the oven on the baking sheet and bake 15 minutes on one side, then flip and bake another 15 minutes. Remove from the oven and place on a wire rack to cool for at least 10 minutes. Burgers are even better after sitting for about 30 minutes.

Make the sauce: Peel and finely mince the garlic. Chop the dill. Juice the lemon. In a small bowl, stir together the garlic, dill, lemon juice, Greek yogurt, olive oil, kosher salt, and 2 tablespoons water. Store leftovers in a sealed container in the refrigerator for 1 to 2 weeks.

To serve, thinly slice cucumber and tomato. Toast the English muffins. Place each burger on an English muffin, and top with cucumber, tomato, and a large dollop of Yogurt Dill Sauce.

Notes

Storage: Leftover burgers can be refrigerated or frozen; they reheat well for quick dinners. Store the burgers refrigerated for up to 5 days, or frozen in an airtight container or plastic bag. To reheat, heat straight from the refrigerator or freezer in a 375°F oven until crispy and heated through; about 8 minutes for refrigerated burgers and about 15 minutes for frozen burgers.

The yogurt sauce makes enough for leftovers; if desired, make half or use leftover sauce as a dip for vegetables or pita.

GF* For gluten-free, use gluten-free flour and gluten-free muffins.

V* For vegan, use Lemon Tahini Drizzle (page 200) instead of Yogurt Dill Sauce.

Giant Portobello Burgers

with Caramelized Onions

People sometimes mistake us for hardcore vegetarians since we eat so many vegetables. In truth, we do indulge in a juicy beef burger once in a while. But for our everyday cooking, we like this burger (almost) as much. This messy sandwich uses the meatiest of all vegetables: the portobello, a thick, juicy mushroom that's not at all like the slimy canned ones I came to fear in childhood. Grilled with a bit of garlic and balsamic, a smoky umami infuses the entire mushroom. To top this special burger, onions are reduced to a dark, sweet caramel mess that tastes like pure gold. You can customize the other toppings to your liking; here we've used a pile of vegetables and smoked cheese. The resulting sandwich is gigantic and a bit messy to handle, but the experience of eating it can't be beat.

FOR THE CARAMELIZED ONIONS

- 3 large Vidalia onions (about 3 pounds)
- 2 tablespoons extra-virgin olive oil
- 1 teaspoon kosher salt

FOR THE MUSHROOMS

- 6 medium portobello mushroom caps
- 2 medium garlic cloves
- 3 tablespoons extra-virgin olive oil
- 2 tablespoons balsamic vinegar
- ½ teaspoon kosher salt
  Freshly ground black pepper
- 1 yellow bell pepper
- 1 red bell pepper

FOR SERVING

- 3 ounces smoked Gruyère or Gouda cheese
- 1 avocado
- 1 large ripe tomato
- 1 red onion
- 2 cups arugula, loosely packed
- 6 hamburger buns
  Freshly ground black pepper

Caramelize the onions: Peel, halve, and thinly slice the onions.

In a very large skillet, heat the olive oil over medium-high heat. Add the onions, which may just fit the skillet and can be mounded if necessary. Sauté, stirring frequently, for about 10 minutes until soft and translucent.

Add the kosher salt and reduce the heat to medium low, finding a temperature that is not so hot that the onions burn but not so low that they do not continue to cook. Cook slowly, stirring every 5 to 10 minutes or so, until reduced and dark brown, about 40 minutes. The onions will turn from translucent white to golden to a rich, dark brown color, and the volume will reduce by at least four times.

Grill the mushrooms and peppers: Preheat a grill to medium high (for an alternative roasting method, see Notes).

Brush any dirt from the mushroom caps and remove the stems. Place the mushrooms gill-side up on a baking sheet. Peel and mince the garlic. Sprinkle the garlic onto the mushrooms, then drizzle each cap with about ½ tablespoon olive oil and 1 teaspoon balsamic vinegar. Add a generous pinch of kosher salt to each (about ½ teaspoon in total) and several grinds of black pepper to each mushroom.

For the bell peppers, turn each pepper on its side and cut off top. Remove pith and seeds, then slice the pepper along its cut side into ¼-inch rings. Slice the cheese.

Place the mushrooms gill side up on the hot grill over direct heat. Place the pepper rings along the edges of the grill over indirect heat. Grill the mushrooms until tender and juicy, about 12 to 15 minutes, then flip, draining any juices, and grill an additional 2 minutes. If desired, flip one more time and melt sliced cheese

onto the mushrooms. Meanwhile, cook the peppers until tender, about 15 minutes. If desired, place the peppers over direct heat toward the end of the cooking time to blacken them.

To serve, slice the avocado, tomato, and red onion and wash the arugula. Serve the portobellos on buns topped with grilled peppers, avocado, tomato, red onion, arugula, and caramelized onions.

Notes

Alternative method: Preheat the oven to 450°F. Line a rimmed baking sheet with parchment paper or a silicone mat. Place the mushrooms gill-side up on the sheet and prepare with garlic, olive oil, balsamic vinegar, and salt as instructed. Add ½ teaspoon liquid smoke to each mushroom. Slice the bell peppers as noted, then place them on the same baking sheet. Roast for
15 minutes until tender. Drain of any excess liquid as necessary.

GF* For gluten-free, use gluten-free buns.

V* For vegan, omit the cheese or use a vegan variety.

Red & Green Enchiladas

On a spring trip to Santa Fe, New Mexico, we stumbled across "Christmas" enchiladas made with both red and green sauces. Intrigued, we set out to re-create our own version. Though it takes a bit of time to prepare, it's visually stunning, extremely flavorful, and ultimately simple—both sauces are whizzed in a blender with no need to precook. The ingredient list is deceptively long; many of them are reused or are common spices that are likely to be on hand. The traditional Mexican ingredients can be found in the international aisle in most grocery stores: green chiles, tomatillos (small green, citrusy tomatoes), and adobo sauce. Toasting the corn tortillas in a bit of oil prior to baking brings out maximum flavor. It's a fitting recipe to prep with a family member or friend, which makes for more fun and less mess.

GF | *Serves* **4 TO 6**

FOR THE FILLING

- 3 cups diced sweet potatoes (about 1 pound)
- ⅓ cup minced red onion (1 small)
- ½ cup chopped cilantro
- 1 15-ounce can black beans
- 1 4-ounce can diced mild green chiles
- 1 teaspoon cumin
- ½ teaspoon garlic powder
- ½ teaspoon kosher salt

FOR THE RED SAUCE

- 2 small garlic cloves
- 1 15-ounce can tomato sauce
- 2 tablespoons tomato paste
- 1 tablespoon adobo sauce (from 1 can chipotle peppers in adobo sauce)*
- 1 teaspoon chili powder
- 1 teaspoon cumin
- 1 teaspoon dried oregano
- ¼ teaspoon kosher salt

Ingredients continue on next page

Preheat the oven to 375°F.

Make the filling: Wash the sweet potatoes, leaving the skin on, then dice them into ½-inch cubes. Place them in a saucepan and fill the pot with cold water 1 inch above the potatoes. Bring to a boil and cook until tender, around 6 to 8 minutes, then drain.

Peel and mince the red onion. Chop the cilantro. Drain and rinse the black beans. In a large bowl, combine the cooked sweet potato, red onion, cilantro, black beans, green chiles, cumin, garlic powder, and kosher salt. Mix to combine.

Make the red sauce: Peel the garlic. In a blender, add the garlic, tomato sauce, tomato paste, adobo sauce, chili powder, cumin, oregano, and kosher salt. Blend on high until fully combined. Transfer to a 2-cup liquid measure or bowl.

Make the green sauce: Wash out the blender. Peel the garlic. Slice the jalapeño pepper in half and remove the ribs and seeds, taking care to properly shield your hands and eyes. Drain the tomatillos. Chop the cilantro. Add the garlic, ½ the jalapeño pepper, tomatillos, green chiles, spinach, cilantro, cumin, onion powder, oregano, and kosher salt. Blend on high until fully combined.

Toast the tortillas: Brush both sides of each tortilla lightly with olive oil. Heat a large griddle to medium-high heat. Cook the tortillas in batches for 15 seconds per side until lightly browned.

Bake the enchiladas: Stir 1 cup cheese into the sweet potato mixture. In a 13 x 9-inch baking dish, spread a thin layer of the red sauce lengthwise on one half of the dish, and then spread a thin layer of the green sauce on the other half. Place a tortilla on a plate and spread ⅓ cup of the filling on the bottom third, then tightly roll it up. Repeat for all tortillas, placing each seam-side down in the

baking dish, with 10 tortillas in the middle and 2 lengthwise on each side for a total of 14 tortillas. Sprinkle the entire pan with a thin layer of cheese, then top each half lengthwise with the remaining red and green sauces. Where the sauces meet in the center, spread the remaining cheese in a line down the middle. Sprinkle the entire pan with torn cilantro leaves. Place in the oven and bake for 20 minutes, until the cheese is melted, then serve warm.

Notes

*Use 1 tablespoon adobo sauce from the can; the peppers and remaining sauce can be reserved (or frozen) for future use.

If desired, serve with sour cream or crème fraîche (page 139).

Make ahead: Make the filling and sauces in advance, then assemble the day of baking.

FOR THE GREEN SAUCE

- 2 small garlic cloves
- 1 jalapeño pepper
- 1 11-ounce can tomatillos
- 1 handful cilantro
- 1 4-ounce can diced mild green chiles
- 3 cups baby spinach leaves, loosely packed (chopped if leaves are large)
- ½ teaspoon cumin
- ½ teaspoon onion powder
- ½ teaspoon dried oregano
- ¼ teaspoon kosher salt

FOR THE ENCHILADAS

- 14 6-inch yellow corn or corn-wheat blend tortillas
- 2 cups shredded Monterey jack cheese (about 8 ounces), divided
- 1 handful cilantro, for garnish
  Mexican hot sauce, to serve

The Best Veggie Lasagna

While "the best" is a bit overused, we feel justified using it here since this recipe has been eaten by dozens of people who have confirmed it is indeed the best vegetarian lasagna. It's creamy and lush, yet light enough to eat without feeling overstuffed. Rich crème fraîche is balanced with bright lemon and the nutrients of leafy greens. Although it takes around two hours start to finish, the concept is pretty simple. It's a brilliant dish that's absolutely worth the effort.

GF* | *Serves* **6 TO 8**

- 1 tablespoon (for the pasta water) plus 1¾ teaspoons kosher salt, divided
- 10 lasagna noodles (8 ounces)
- 6 medium garlic cloves
- 1½ teaspoons red pepper flakes
- 2 tablespoons unsalted butter
- 1 28-ounce can crushed tomatoes
- 1 15-ounce can tomato sauce
- 1 teaspoon dried basil
- 1 teaspoon dried oregano
- Freshly ground black pepper
- 1 teaspoon lemon juice and 2 teaspoons zest (½ lemon), divided
- 2–3 medium bunches rainbow chard (about 1½ pounds)
- 1 tablespoon extra-virgin olive oil
- 2½ tablespoons chopped fresh thyme, divided
- 1½ cups (12 ounces) crème fraîche (page 139 or purchased)
- 1 cup grated Parmesan cheese, divided
- 3 cups shredded mozzarella cheese, divided
- ¼ teaspoon ground nutmeg

Preheat the oven to 375°F. Drizzle a baking sheet with a bit of olive oil and set aside.

Boil the noodles: Bring a large pot of water to boil with 1 tablespoon kosher salt. Boil the noodles until just al dente, according to the package instructions, stirring often. Drain the noodles. Lay them flat onto the oiled baking sheet, and turn them over so they become coated with olive oil to prevent sticking.

Prepare the sauce: Peel and mince the garlic. Add the garlic, red pepper flakes, and butter to a saucepan and bring to medium heat, stirring frequently. Once the garlic is lightly browned and fragrant after about 2 minutes, turn down the heat and carefully add the crushed tomatoes, tomato sauce, basil, oregano, ¾ teaspoon kosher salt, and several grinds of black pepper. Cover the pan, then simmer while making the remainder of the recipe, around 20 minutes. When ready to use, remove the pan from the heat and stir in 1 teaspoon lemon juice.

Sauté the chard: Destem the chard by holding the leaf at the lowest part of the stem and pulling back to tear the leaf away from the stem, then roughly chop the leaves. In a large skillet, heat the olive oil over medium heat. Mound the greens in the skillet and sauté, stirring often, until completely wilted and reduced, about 3 to 4 minutes. (The greens significantly reduce when cooking; if necessary, sauté in 2 batches.) Sprinkle 2 pinches of kosher salt and stir; remove from the heat and allow to cool slightly. Once cooled, use your hands to squeeze out all excess liquid from the chard.

Prepare the cheese filling: Destem the thyme and chop the leaves. Add 2 tablespoons of chopped thyme to a medium bowl and reserve ½ tablespoon for topping the lasagna. To the bowl, add

the crème fraîche, ¾ cup Parmesan cheese, 2 cups mozzarella cheese, 2 teaspoons lemon zest, nutmeg, 1 teaspoon kosher salt, and several grinds of black pepper. Stir to combine.

Bake the lasagna: In a 13 x 9-inch baking dish, spread a thin layer of tomato sauce on the bottom of the pan. Then top with 1 layer of noodles, half of the cheese mixture (in dollops), half of the greens, and about one third of the tomato sauce. Repeat again: 1 layer of noodles, the remaining cheese mixture, the remaining greens, and half of the remaining tomato sauce. Finally, top with noodles (you may need to slice the tenth noodle in half for the top layer), then the rest of the tomato sauce. Sprinkle the entire top with the remaining 1 cup mozzarella cheese, ¼ cup Parmesan cheese, and ½ tablespoon thyme.

Cover the pan with aluminum foil and bake for 40 minutes. Carefully remove the foil and bake another 15 minutes, until bubbly and browned. Let stand for 15 minutes before serving.

Notes

Storage: Leftovers can be refrigerated for 2 to 3 days and reheated in a 375°F oven.

If you're looking for a crowd-pleasing Italian dish to make in half the time, see Ricotta Gnocchi alla Vodka (page 208).

GF* For gluten-free, use gluten-free noodles.

Classic Vegetarian Nut Loaf

This recipe is a showstopper that satisfies even the most meat-forward of eaters. Tested and beloved by our readers across the country, this nut roast really does taste like a savory, chewy meat loaf. My mother is a passionate meat lover and literally begs us to make this at the holidays. It's an adaptation of a concept from Deborah Madison in *The Greens Cookbook*, and we've added a ketchup-like tomato glaze. While the concept is pretty simple, the execution requires about 2 hours to pull off. For a special occasion, it's absolutely worth the effort. For weeknight dinners, consider freezing any leftovers—or follow the make-ahead instructions for a quicker prep. And if you're not a mushroom lover, we've had dozens of people tell us it's the first time they've liked mushrooms in a dish.

GF | *Serves 8*

FOR THE NUT LOAF

- 1½ cups cooked brown rice
- 1 cup raw walnuts
- 1 cup raw cashews
- 1¼ cups minced red onion (1 medium)
- 3 medium garlic cloves
- 8 ounces baby bella (cremini) mushrooms
- 2 tablespoons finely chopped Italian flat-leaf parsley
- 12 ounces Swiss cheese
- 2 tablespoons extra-virgin olive oil
- 1 teaspoon dried oregano
- 1 teaspoon dried thyme
- 1 teaspoon dried sage
- 4 large eggs
- 1 cup cottage cheese
- 1 teaspoon kosher salt
- ½ teaspoon freshly ground black pepper

FOR THE GLAZE

- 1 cup tomato sauce
- 2 teaspoons Dijon mustard
- 4 teaspoons honey
- 2 teaspoons balsamic vinegar
- ¼ teaspoon chili powder
- 2 pinches garlic powder
- 2 pinches kosher salt

Cook the brown rice (page 136).

Meanwhile, preheat the oven to 375°F.

Assemble the nut loaf: Place the walnuts and cashews on a baking sheet and bake for 5 to 8 minutes until lightly browned. Cool slightly, then finely chop.

Peel and mince the onion. Peel and mince the garlic, then place the onion and garlic in a bowl. Brush any dirt from the mushrooms. Remove and discard the stems; finely chop the caps and set aside. Finely chop the parsley and set aside. Grate the Swiss cheese and set aside.

In a large skillet, heat the olive oil over medium-high heat. Add the onion and garlic and sauté until translucent, about 3 minutes. Add the mushrooms, oregano, thyme, and sage. Continue to sauté until the mushrooms are golden and fragrant, about 5 minutes. Remove from the heat and allow to cool slightly.

In a large bowl, lightly beat the eggs. Add the sautéed mushroom mixture, parsley, chopped nuts, cottage cheese, Swiss cheese, 1½ cups cooked rice, kosher salt, and black pepper, and stir to combine.

Start the baking: Grease a 9-inch loaf pan, line the bottom with parchment paper, and butter the top of the parchment paper. Pour the mixture from the bowl into the loaf pan and bake for 45 minutes.

Make the glaze: Meanwhile, in a small bowl, stir together the tomato sauce, mustard, honey, balsamic vinegar, chili powder, garlic powder, and kosher salt.

Finish the baking: Remove the loaf from the oven and brush it with roughly half of the glaze; reserve the remainder for serving. Then return to the oven for another 15 minutes until golden brown and firm, for a total of 1 hour baking time. Remove from the oven and allow to cool in the pan for at least 20 minutes, then run a knife around the edges and remove slices from the pan. If you have the time, the loaf will firm up nicely if allowed to rest for a few more minutes. Serve warm or at room temperature, with the remaining glaze on the side.

Notes

Make ahead: Make the rice, sauté the vegetables, and toast and chop the nuts in advance. Store the rice and cooked vegetables covered in the refrigerator and the toasted nuts in a sealed container at room temperature, prior to assembling the loaf.

Storage: Slice the loaf and place the slices in an airtight plastic bag, laying the slices flat, then freeze. To reheat, place the slices on a baking sheet and reheat in a 375°F oven for about 20 minutes, until warmed through.

Artisan Pizza: Three Ways

The entire plane ride home from our honeymoon in Italy, Alex and I were abuzz with an idea: learning to make the artisan-style pizza we had eaten in Rome. We'd start a pizzeria with a fancy Italian name—Il Foro, in honor of the Roman forum—and learn to make that tender crust, that silky red tomato sauce, that sexy, salty cheese, and those minimalist toppings. Oh, and serve it with traditional Italian gelato.

Ten years later we've finally mastered the craft of Italian-style artisan pizza. The restaurant dream fell by the wayside—but honestly, we'd much rather spend our time making this pizza for friends and family (and ourselves). We're excited to reveal our secrets so that you can, too.

While pizza is not usually listed as a health food, artisan-style Italian pizza is a different animal than the American version. With a thin crust and a moderate amount of cheese, this is not the greasy carbo-loaded American kind. And since it takes a bit of effort to make at home, it's not meant to be an everyday meal. In our household, pizza is always a celebration food, whether it's a Pizza Friday with a kitchen full of friends, or an intimate dinner for just the two of us.

Making pizza at home is an art that requires a bit of time, the right tools, and a whole lot of practice. If you don't get it right the first time, try, try again. It took us 10 years to master this, and we hope with these tricks, it will take you much less time!

Get a pizza stone and a pizza peel. A pizza stone is essential for achieving a crispy crust in a standard home oven, which can only get up to around 500°F (most wood-fired ovens use 800°F or higher). A pizza peel is a wooden tray with a handle used to slide the pizza onto and off of the pizza stone; it's a must.

Quality of ingredients is key. What we've learned from the Italians: use top-quality ingredients. For perfect dough, we recommend Tipo "00" flour, the finest grade of flour milled in Italy. Pizzerias use it to achieve a fluffy, supple dough. Canned San Marzano tomatoes, a variety of tomato from Italy, are traditionally used on pizzas for their sweet, nuanced taste. They're now becoming widely available in grocery stores in America or online.

Simple is best. What we love about Italian pizza is its simplicity—just a handful of complimentary toppings are used per pizza. When we first started making pizza the Italian way, we were surprised at how little we used of each ingredient, especially tomatoes and cheese. Using ingredients sparingly allows each one to shine.

Pizza Dough

450 grams (about 3 cups) flour,
    Tipo "00" if possible*

  2 teaspoons (1 packet) instant yeast

  2 teaspoons extra-virgin olive oil

  ½ teaspoon kosher salt

315 grams (1⅓ cups) warm water
    Cornmeal, for baking**

This dough recipe is our original method, honed from years of pizza making. A trick we learned from the chef at our favorite stateside artisan pizza joint, Pizzicletta in Flagstaff, Arizona, is allowing the dough to rest for a few days in the refrigerator before baking. It yields a complex, nutty flavor that's worth the wait. You can knead the dough by hand, or use a dough hook on a stand mixer; both work equally well. Stretching the dough takes quite a bit of practice, so don't worry if your first several pizzas don't come out quite as you imagined.

Hand-kneading method: Combine the flour, yeast, olive oil, kosher salt, and water in a bowl and mix with a wooden spoon until just combined. Turn the dough out onto a clean, lightly floured countertop. Using your hands, start to form the dough into a ball; at first it will be rather floury, and then after 30 seconds it will become quite sticky. Resist the urge to add too much extra flour unless the stickiness is unbearable. Knead the dough by pushing with the base of your palm, then reforming it into a ball. Continue kneading for 8 to 10 minutes until the dough feels pillowy and has a smooth, stretchy exterior.

Stand mixer method: In the bowl of a stand mixer, add the flour, yeast, olive oil, kosher salt, and water. Using the dough hook from the mixer, stir until a loose dough forms. Attach the dough hook to the mixer and start the mixer on medium-low speed, then allow the mixer to knead for 8 minutes. The dough should be rather sticky; if it forms into a hard ball, add a teaspoon of water.

After the kneading is finished, divide the dough in half. Using floured hands, gently shape each half into a boule (ball shape) by folding the dough under itself. Set each boule on a floured surface and dab it with a bit of olive oil to keep it moist. Cover both boules with a damp towel and allow them to rise for 45 minutes to 1 hour, until roughly doubled in size.

Transfer the dough to separate sealed containers, large enough for the dough to double in size again, and keep it in the refrigerator for 3 days: this ferments the dough and creates a rich, slightly sour crust. (Alternatively, you can use the dough immediately after the initial rise, though the taste is not as complex.) The day of serving, remove the dough from the containers, place it on a lightly floured surface covered with a towel, and allow it to come to room temperature before stretching, 30 to 45 minutes.

To stretch the dough, place it on a lightly floured surface and gently press it into a circle, flipping several times and adding a pinch of flour if it is too sticky. Once you have about an 8-inch circle, pick up the dough and gently drape it over the knuckles on both of your hands. Slowly rotate it around, allowing gravity to stretch it into a circle. Do not overwork or fold the dough. If the dough starts to resist stretching, put it down and allow it to rest for a few minutes, at which point it will stretch more easily.

To bake, about 30 minutes before the pizza dough is ready, preheat the oven with a pizza stone at 500°F. Sprinkle a bit of cornmeal onto a pizza peel (or rimless baking sheet). Place the stretched dough onto the peel and quickly add the desired toppings, then transfer to the pizza stone and bake 7 to 8 minutes until browned.

Notes

Storage: If only using one dough, you can freeze the other for later use in an airtight plastic bag. The morning you plan to use the dough, remove it from the freezer and place it in the refrigerator to thaw. About 30 to 45 minutes before making the pizza, take the dough out of the bag and allow it to relax on the counter, covered with a towel.

*Weigh out the flour if possible, since the density of the flour depends on the environment and the cup measurement can vary. If you don't have a food scale, use 3 cups and adjust the water and/or flour to come the right consistency.

**If you make pizza often, we recommend the Super Peel model of a pizza peel, which has a canvas cloth conveyor belt that makes for an easy slide onto the pizza stone. In this case, you can omit the cornmeal.

Pizza Margherita

with Pecorino & Egg

Makes **1 MEDIUM PIZZA**

On our honeymoon in Rome, we made sure to visit the restaurant that our guidebook promised served "the best pizza in Italy." A few things surprised us newbies: first, we were seated at a table with a couple of strangers, and second, our pizza came with an egg on top. What wasn't a surprise: it was some damn good pizza. The richness of the egg yolk against the sweetness of the tomatoes was spot on, and we've been making pizza with egg ever since. This one is a fancied-up take on pizza margherita, the classic tomato, mozzarella, and basil pie; we add eggs and wilted green onions. Using San Marzano tomatoes, a delicately sweet Italian variety, is a must on a great margherita. Instead of making a sauce, we use the crushed tomatoes straight from the can and top them with minced garlic and a bit of salt. We also love adding finely grated Pecorino cheese over the mozzarella, a hard Italian cheese similar to Parmesan with a sharper flavor.

1 pizza dough (page 224)

2 medium garlic cloves

4 green onions

½ tablespoon extra-virgin olive oil, plus more for brushing

⅔ cup crushed San Marzano tomatoes
Kosher salt

½ cup shredded mozzarella cheese

½ cup shredded Pecorino cheese

2 eggs

5 basil leaves

Make the pizza dough (page 224).

Place a pizza stone in the oven and preheat to 500°F.

Peel and mince the garlic and reserve it. Slice the dark green parts from the green onions. In a small skillet, heat ½ tablespoon olive oil. Add the onion greens and sauté until tender and wilted, about 2 minutes. Remove from the heat.

When the oven is heated, stretch the dough into a circle. Place the dough on a pizza peel sprinkled with a bit of cornmeal (for more detail, see page 225).

Brush the entire dough with a light coating of olive oil. Spread the tomatoes over the dough, then sprinkle with the minced garlic and a few pinches of kosher salt. Sprinkle the dough with the mozzarella cheese, then add the Pecorino cheese and arrange the green onions on top. Carefully crack two eggs onto the pizza, and sprinkle with another small pinch of kosher salt.

Transfer the pizza to the oven on the pizza peel. Bake until the egg white is set and the yolk is still runny, watching carefully toward the end of the cooking time. Depending on the oven, this can take anywhere from 7 to 12 minutes. Remove from the oven and cool for a few minutes. Slice the basil into thin strips. Sprinkle the pizza with basil, slice into pieces, and serve warm.

This pizza is all about summertime's crown jewel: juicy heirloom tomatoes. Our summer farmers' market boasts tomatoes of all sizes and colors: bright yellow, chartreuse striped, salmon, and scarlet. To showcase the vibrant colors, toppings on this "white" pizza are added directly to the dough without tomato sauce. Topped with creamy goat cheese, fresh thyme, and red onion slivers, it's little bit of heaven in pizza form.

Pizza
with Heirloom Tomatoes & Goat Cheese

V* | *Makes* **1 MEDIUM PIZZA**

1 pizza dough (page 224)

¼ cup sliced red onion (1 small)

2 teaspoons chopped fresh thyme

3 small multicolored heirloom tomatoes (about ½–¾ pound)

Extra-virgin olive oil

¾ cup shredded mozzarella cheese

2 ounces soft goat cheese

Kosher salt

Make the pizza dough (page 224).

Place a pizza stone in the oven and preheat to 500°F.

Peel and thinly slice the red onion into crescent shapes, slicing from the top end to the root end. Roughly chop the thyme leaves. Place the tomatoes on their sides and use a sharp, serrated knife to cut into rounds about ⅛-inch thick. Avoid using thick slices, which will cause the pizza dough to become soggy.

When the oven is heated, stretch the dough into a circle. Place the dough on a pizza peel sprinkled with a bit of cornmeal (for more detail, see page 225).

Brush the entire dough with a light coating of olive oil. Sprinkle the dough with the mozzarella cheese, then place the tomatoes on top. Top with red onions, thyme, and small dollops of goat cheese. Sprinkle the entire pizza with kosher salt (especially the tomatoes, which need a good salting).

Bake until the mozzarella cheese is melted and the crust is golden brown, watching carefully toward the end of the cooking time. Depending on the oven, this can take anywhere from 7 to 12 minutes. Remove from the oven and cool for a few minutes, then cut into pieces and serve warm.

V* For vegan, consider a high-quality vegan cheese; ask your grocer for recommendations.

Pizza

with Sweet Potatoes & Smoked Garlic

As you'll notice throughout this book, Alex and I are big fans of smoky flavor. Alex's passion for smoking meat inspired him to create this method for smoking garlic. It ends up tasting like pure smoke—and only takes about 30 minutes in a homemade smoker made from two disposable aluminum baking pans. This pizza is a sophisticated meatless version of chicken barbecue pizza, with smoky bits of garlic, roasted sweet potatoes, and chard ribbons. While smoking garlic is not an everyday technique, it's a pretty simple way to add a gourmet touch.

1 pizza dough (page 224)

FOR THE SMOKED GARLIC

5 medium garlic cloves

1 tablespoon hickory or cherry stovetop smoking chips (or 4–5 small standard smoking chips)*

1 bowl-shaped disposable aluminum potpie pan

1 rectangular disposable aluminum baking pan, 3 to 4 inches deep

FOR THE PIZZA

1 small sweet potato (6–8 ounces)

1 teaspoon extra-virgin olive oil, plus more for brushing

¼ teaspoon kosher salt, plus more for sprinkling

2 large chard leaves

⅔ cup crushed San Marzano tomatoes

¾ cup mozzarella cheese

Parmesan cheese, grated

Make the pizza dough (page 224).

Smoke the garlic: Peel the garlic cloves. Using a fork or knife, poke several holes in the bottom of the bowl-shaped aluminum potpie pan.

Place the rectangular aluminum baking pan on a small stovetop burner. Place the smoking chips in the center of the deep pan, and cover with the potpie pan, inverted so the flat side is up, creating a dome over the chips. Place the garlic on top of the potpie pan.

Cover the top of the rectangular baking pan tightly with aluminum foil, leaving one corner a little loose. Turn on the burner to medium heat until you see smoke escaping from the corner, then quickly secure the corner so the smoke is trapped inside. Turn the heat to low and heat for 20 minutes while enjoying the wafting smoky smell.

After 20 minutes, remove the heat and take the baking pan outdoors to remove the foil and release the smoke. The garlic should be golden brown; remove it from the smoker. Use immediately, or refrigerate until using.

Make the pizza: Place a pizza stone in the oven and preheat to 450°F.

Slice the sweet potato into ¼-inch-thick rounds, leaving the skin on. In a small bowl, mix the slices with the olive oil and kosher salt. Line a baking sheet with parchment paper or a silicone mat, then add the slices in a single layer. Roast until tender when pricked with a fork, about 10 minutes. Remove the baking sheet from the oven; flip the sweet potatoes and allow them to cool.

Destem the chard by holding the leaf at the lowest part of the stem and pulling back to tear the leaf away from the stem, then slice the leaves into thin strips. Mince the smoked garlic.

Turn up the oven to 500°F. When the oven is heated, stretch the dough into a circle. Place the dough on a pizza peel sprinkled with a bit of cornmeal (for more detail, see page 225).

Brush the entire dough with a light coating of olive oil. Spread the tomatoes over the dough, then sprinkle with a few pinches kosher salt. Add the chard ribbons; top with the mozzarella cheese and sprinkle with the smoked garlic. Top with the sweet potato rounds and cover the entire pizza with a bit of freshly grated Parmesan cheese.

Bake until the cheese is melted and the crust is golden brown, watching carefully toward the end of the cooking time. Depending on the oven, this can take anywhere from 7 to 12 minutes. Remove from the oven and cool for a few minutes, then cut into pieces and serve warm.

Notes

*Stovetop smoking chips are sawdust-like in texture and can be found in cooking stores or online.

V* For vegan, consider a high-quality vegan cheese; ask your grocer for recommendations.

"Try new recipes, learn from your mistakes,
be fearless, and above all have fun!"

—JULIA CHILD, *MY LIFE IN FRANCE*

Have fun.

Somewhere along the line, we've lost the fun of it all. We work to pay the bills and cook to fill our bellies. Yes, life is hard and weighty, and in it there is grief and heartache. Some days there is no time for fun, and in some seasons no time for laughter.

But in other seasons, there is a call to play. To remember the lightness of childhood and channel that delight. To free ourselves from all the rules and expectations and weightiness of being human and just have fun. To delight in food, the making it and the sharing it.

Instead of being disappointed in non-perfection, let's embrace the messy ride (and the occasional splatter of tomato sauce). Above all, let's have fun.

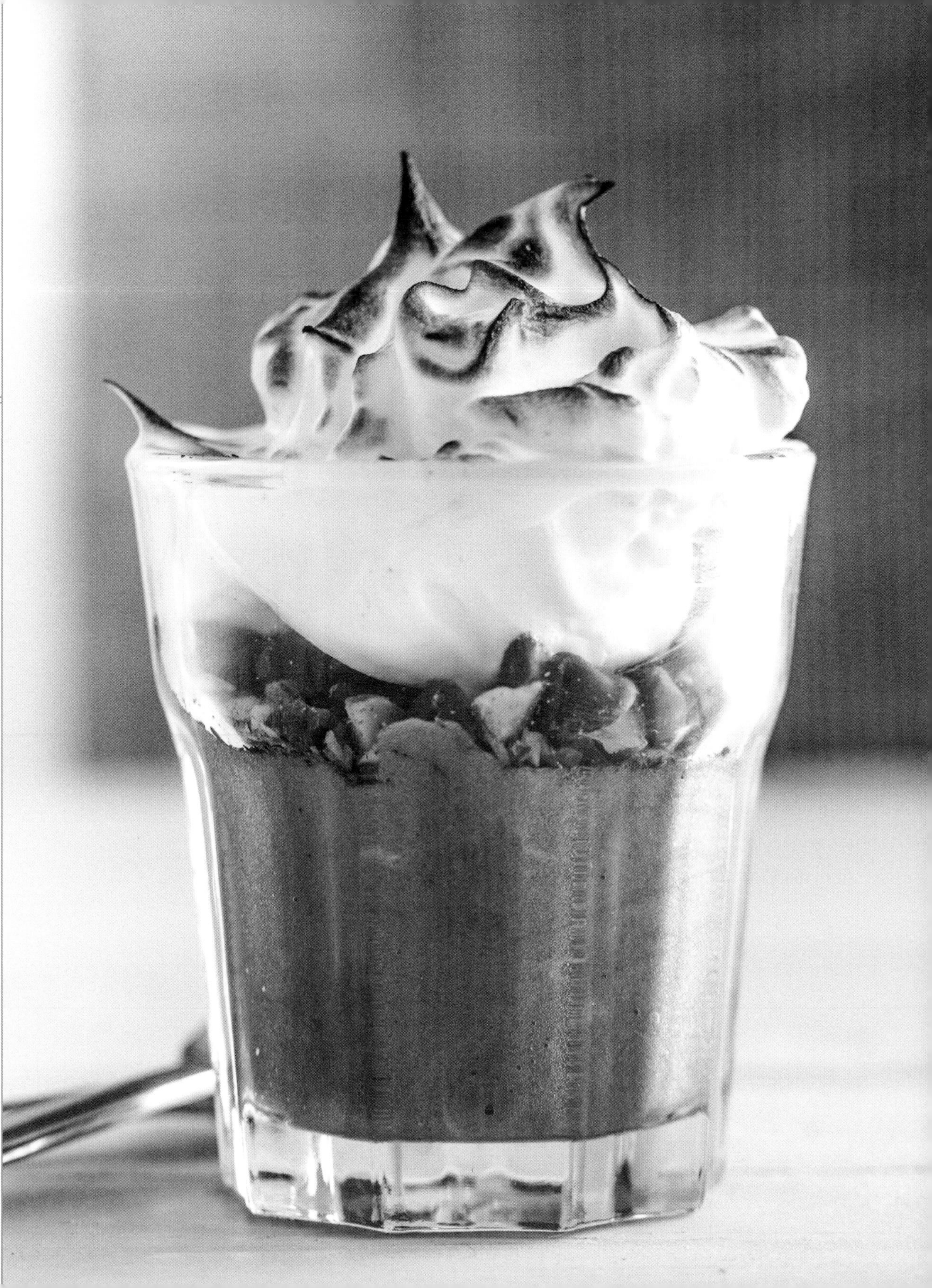

Sweets

Fresh Berries

with Mint & Vanilla Whipped Cream

In Indiana summers, our farmers' markets burst with jewel-toned strawberries, blackberries, blueberries, and raspberries. To us, topping them with lightly sweet homemade whipped cream and fresh mint rivals the world's most elaborate dessert. Alex and I typically whip cream by hand—because in a world where everything is prepackaged and mechanized, we find it personally satisfying to earn our dessert with nothing but a whisk, a bowl, and a carton of cream. Along with mint, we've added a sprinkle of ground cardamom for a hint of exotic fragrance. It's so quick to put together, it's worth having whipping cream or coconut milk on hand in case of a lucky summer farmers' market find.

GF | **V*** | *Serves 4*

1 cup heavy whipping cream

1 tablespoon plus ½ teaspoon pure maple syrup (or confectioners' sugar), divided

½ teaspoon vanilla extract

½ teaspoon finely chopped fresh mint

1 pint fresh seasonal berries of any type

¼ teaspoon balsamic vinegar

Ground cardamom, for garnish

Whip the cream: In a large bowl, combine the heavy cream, 1 tablespoon maple syrup, and vanilla extract. With a large whisk, whip the cream vigorously until it thickens and peaks start to form, 2 to 3 minutes. Whisk to your desired thickness, soft or stiff peaks, taking care not to overwhip or it will turn into butter. It helps to place the bowl in the sink to whip the cream so that it is a bit lower than counter height.

Prepare the berries: Finely chop the mint. In a bowl, toss the berries with the mint, ½ teaspoon maple syrup, and the balsamic vinegar.

To serve, place the berries in small bowls, then top with whipped cream and a pinch of ground cardamom.

Notes

Storage: Extra whipped cream stores for 1 day refrigerated in an airtight container.

For coconut whipped cream: Refrigerate one 15-ounce can full-fat coconut milk overnight. When ready to prepare, open the coconut milk and remove the hardened coconut cream on top, taking care to avoid the liquid in the bottom of the can. Place the cream in the bowl of a stand mixer or a bowl, then discard the remaining liquid or save it for another recipe. Add 1 tablespoon maple syrup and ½ teaspoon vanilla extract. Using the whisk attachment on a stand mixer or electric hand mixer, blend on high for about 1 minute until light and fluffy.

V* For vegan, top with coconut whipped cream.

Here's another trick we picked up from our visits to Italy, and it's one of the simplest, most sumptuous after-dinner treats around. Affogato literally means drowned, referring to the best kind of drowning—vanilla ice cream or gelato in dark, strong coffee. The warm coffee immediately turns the ice cream to a soupy, espresso-y mess. We've added a few touches of our own: a splash of bourbon and the crunch of toasted almonds. If dinner guests show up unannounced, this is our go-to.

Affogato al Caffè

GF | V* | *Serves 4*

2 tablespoons sliced almonds

1 pint high-quality vanilla ice cream

½ cup espresso or strong coffee (decaf if desired)

2 teaspoons bourbon

In a small dry skillet over medium heat, toast the almonds until lightly browned and fragrant, stirring frequently, about 5 minutes. Remove from the heat and set aside.

Add 1 large scoop of ice cream to four serving glasses. Chill in the freezer while preparing the coffee (this helps the ice cream to be as cold as possible when serving).

Make 4 shots of espresso in an espresso maker, or make a strong coffee using your normal method with half of the standard amount of water.

To serve, remove the glasses with the ice cream from the freezer and sprinkle with the toasted almonds. At the table, pour 2 tablespoons espresso and ½ teaspoon bourbon per serving over the ice cream, then serve immediately.

V* For vegan, use vegan ice cream.

Sparkling Amethyst Granita

Comparing mutual interests on a dinner date, Alex and I realized that we both had rock collections growing up (clearly we were meant to be together). This dessert reminds us of the amethyst geodes we both had in our stashes. After blending, freezing, and scraping, a short list of ingredients transforms into sparkling purple crystals. The blueberries, lime, maple, vanilla, and nutmeg morph into something we decided tastes decidedly purple. This is a refreshing dessert to follow Artisan Pizza (page 222), The Best Veggie Lasagna (page 218), or Kale and Goat Cheese Rigatoni (page 160).

GF | **V** | *Serves 4*

2 tablespoons lime juice (1 large lime)
2½ cups (12 ounces) fresh blueberries*
½ cup water
3 tablespoons pure maple syrup
¼ teaspoon vanilla extract
⅛ teaspoon nutmeg

Juice the lime. Combine all of the ingredients in a blender and purée on high for about 1 minute until fully combined into a smooth, dark purple liquid. Taste and adjust lime or maple syrup if desired.

Pour the liquid into a 13 x 9-inch baking dish. Freeze for 2 to 3 hours until mostly hardened, then scrape with a fork into a fluffy, slushy texture. Serve immediately or if desired, freeze until serving. If very icy, thaw slightly before serving.

Notes
Storage: Store in an airtight container for a few days in the freezer.

*If blueberries are not available, substitute 12 ounces frozen mixed berries for a comparable flavor.

The magic in these raw truffles comes from Medjool dates, an exceptionally large variety that lends a gooey texture and rich taste. We've been using these dates for years, with cocoa powder and walnuts, to whip up raw brownies as a wholesome sweet treat. Here we've used the same concept to make round truffles, coating them in finely ground pistachios as a sort of fluorescent yellow-green confetti. They're quick to put together with a food processor, and we store them in the freezer since they thaw almost immediately.

Raw Brownie Truffles

with Pistachio Dust

GF | V | *Makes* **30 TRUFFLES**

¼ cup raw or roasted shelled pistachios

1 cup raw unsalted walnuts

14 large Medjool dates (about 1½ cups)*

½ cup cocoa powder

2 teaspoons vanilla extract

⅛ teaspoon kosher salt

In a food processor, grind the pistachios for a minute or so into a very fine dust. Remove the pistachio dust to a plate or flat dish and set it aside. Wipe out the bowl of the food processor.

Return the bowl to the food processor and add the walnuts; process for a few seconds until very finely chopped. Remove the pits from the dates. Add the dates, cocoa powder, vanilla extract, and salt and process for another few seconds until the mixture is fully combined and crumbly.

Turn out the mixture into a medium bowl. Take a small handful of the mixture, squeeze it together and then roll it between your hands to form a ball, about ¾ inch in diameter. Repeat to make 30 truffles total. Roll each in the plate of pistachio dust, then place the truffles in a sealable container.

Notes

Storage: Store refrigerated or frozen; wait for a few minutes to warm to room temperature before eating.

*Avoid substituting other date varieties and stick with Medjools; they can be found in the produce aisle in supermarkets and online.

Bliss Bites

GF | **V** | *Makes* **24 BITES**

Bliss Bites are hands down our most popular recipe. The term "life-changing" has even been thrown around for these no-bake treats. People often tell us they're a mainstay in their refrigerator or freezer—and a little dangerous to keep around! Luckily, the danger here is a wholesome variety: they're made with no refined sugars or flours, just coconut oil, peanut butter, maple syrup, cocoa powder, and oats. Essentially an inside-out mini peanut butter cup, they're simple to put together—and pretty blissful.

- 6 tablespoons coconut oil, divided
- 6 tablespoons peanut butter, divided
- 5 tablespoons pure maple syrup, divided
- ¼ cup Dutch process or dark cocoa powder*
- 1 teaspoon vanilla extract
- 1 pinch kosher salt
- 1 cup plus 2 tablespoons rolled oats

Place cupcake liners into a 24-cup mini-muffin tin.

Make the bites: In a small saucepan over low heat, whisk together 5 tablespoons coconut oil, 2 tablespoons peanut butter, 4 tablespoons maple syrup, cocoa powder, vanilla extract, and kosher salt, until fully combined. Remove from the heat and stir in the oats. Spoon about 2 teaspoons of the oat mixture into the bottom of each cupcake liner, then freeze the tin while making the peanut butter glaze.

Make the glaze: Wash the saucepan and return it to the stove. Over low heat, whisk together 1 tablespoon coconut oil, 4 tablespoons peanut butter, and 1 tablespoon maple syrup until fully combined. Remove the tin from the freezer and spoon the warm peanut butter mixture over the top of the chocolate oat mixture. Return the tin to the freezer for 15 minutes until the bites are set, or refrigerate until serving.

Notes
Storage: Store refrigerated or frozen.

For a twist, chop the bliss bites and serve them over vanilla ice cream.

*Standard cocoa powder can be substituted if dark is unavailable.

In our kitchen, we're constantly searching for the intersection of wholesome and delicious—especially with desserts. This skillet cookie is an experiment gone right. It's made with almond flour instead of white flour, making it nutrient-filled and naturally gluten-free. Instead of being overly dense, the texture is soft and chewy. With pockets of rich dark chocolate and just the right amount of sea salt, our family and friends find it hard to resist. You can serve it warm from the oven in wedges, or make it in advance and store the pieces in a cookie jar. The 30-minute rest time makes certain the texture is set—but if you just can't wait, enjoy it with forks directly from the skillet.

Dark Chocolate Sea Salt Skillet Cookie

GF | *Makes **8 SLICES***

Preheat the oven to 400°F.

Chop the chocolate into chunks.

In a medium bowl, mix together the almond flour, brown sugar, and kosher salt. Stir in the melted butter, egg white, vanilla extract, and the majority of the chocolate chunks (reserve a small handful for pressing into the top). Stir until combined, then use your hands to form the dough into a ball.

Press the dough into an even layer in an 8-inch nonstick skillet, then press the remaining chocolate chunks into the top. Smooth the top by rolling over it with a small glass. Sprinkle with sea salt flakes, crushing them with your fingers as you sprinkle.

Bake 18 to 20 minutes until golden brown at the edges. Allow to cool for 30 minutes so that the texture sets but the cookie is still warm. Slice into wedges and serve, or if desired, carefully run a thin knife around the edge and invert the entire cookie onto a plate, then flip it right-side up onto a serving plate.

Notes
Storage: If desired, cut into pieces and store the cookies in an airtight container at room temperature for up to 1 week or frozen for up to 2 months.

*Do not use almond meal, which is coarser and made from almonds with skins. Almond flour is ground more finely and is made with blanched almonds, which have no skins.

For dairy-free, use coconut oil in place of the butter.

- 2 ounces high-quality dark chocolate
- ¼ cup unsalted butter, melted
- 2 cups almond flour*
- 6 tablespoons packed light brown sugar
- ¼ teaspoon kosher salt
- 1 egg white
- 1 teaspoon vanilla extract
- ¼ teaspoon flaky sea salt (we like Maldon)

Flourless Dark Chocolate Cake

with Macerated Raspberries

This cake is rich and fudgy, a chocolate lover's dream. But for all its richness, it's made of just a few whole food ingredients, sweetened with pure maple syrup, and naturally gluten-free. Best of all, it's simple to put together: melt chocolate, mix in the remaining ingredients, and bake. Instead of pairing the cake with a sauce that involves blending or straining, we've chosen the simplest technique of all: macerating, where the berries are mixed with sweetener and set out at room temperature until they naturally break down into a sweet sauce. This is our pick for the grand finale of a dinner party or a treat to wow a special someone.

GF | *Serves* **10 TO 12**

FOR THE CAKE

- 6 ounces 60% bittersweet chocolate (1 cup chips)
- ½ cup (1 stick) unsalted butter
- ½ cup pure maple syrup
- ½ cup cocoa powder, plus more for dusting
- 3 large eggs

FOR THE MACERATED RASPBERRIES

- 6 ounces raspberries
- 2 tablespoons pure maple syrup
- 1 teaspoon lime juice
- ¼ teaspoon vanilla extract

Notes

Storage: Cool completely, then place the cake in a sealed plastic bag and freeze for up to 1 month. To thaw, place in the refrigerator for several hours until thawed.

Preheat the oven to 375°F.

Bake the cake: Cut a sheet of parchment paper into a circle to fit the bottom of an 8-inch springform pan, then place the parchment circle in the pan. Grease the entire pan, including the parchment paper.

Place the chocolate and butter in a glass measuring cup. Fill a large skillet halfway with water and heat to a slow simmer. Once the water is simmering, turn off the heat, place the measuring cup in the water, and stir until the chocolate is fully melted.

Once the chocolate is melted, pour it into a bowl; gradually stir in the maple syrup, then the cocoa powder. Whisk in each of the eggs, one by one, until the batter is silky and dark.

Pour the batter into the prepared pan and smooth it into an even layer with a spatula. Bake around 25 minutes until the middle is just set. Cool in the pan on a wire rack until the cake reaches room temperature, about 1 hour, then refrigerate for at least 1 hour. Before serving, carefully remove the springform pan sides. Invert the cake onto a plate, and gently remove the parchment from the bottom. Revert the cake onto a serving platter and dust with cocoa powder.

Macerate the raspberries: Prior to serving, place the raspberries in a small bowl with the maple syrup, lime juice, and vanilla extract, and let sit for 30 minutes to 1 hour or more, gently stirring occasionally. The raspberries will break down and become syrupy the longer they sit.

To serve, cut the cake into slices and top with macerated raspberries.

A craggy apple tree anchored my backyard growing up. Each fall my family would pick the sweet-tart fruit and make loads of applesauce, apple butter, and apple crisp. This crumble is a wholesome version of the traditional recipe I grew up on, taken to new heights. Tangy, caramelly apples are punctuated with tart cherries and topped with crunchy pecans and oats. It's naturally vegan and gluten-free by way of coconut oil and oat flour, and has significantly less sugar than my family recipe without losing any flavor. If time allows, use our home-made crème fraîche for a creamy maple topping; it's simple to pull together and out-of-this-world good.

Apple Cherry Cardamom Crumble

GF* | **V*** | *Serves 8*

Preheat the oven to 350°F.

Make the filling: Peel the apples and thinly slice them. In a medium bowl, stir together apples, lemon zest, brown sugar, cinnamon, cardamom, cherries, and cornstarch.

Make the crumble: If necessary, make the oat flour by blending 1 cup rolled oats in a food processor or high speed blender until finely ground. In a medium bowl, combine the oat flour, rolled oats, kosher salt, and pecans. Cut in the coconut oil using a pastry blender, then add the maple syrup and mix until well combined.

Bake the crumble: Place the filling into a 9 x 9-inch baking dish, then spread the crumble over the top. Bake until golden brown, 50 to 55 minutes.

Make the topping: While the crumble bakes, mix together the crème fraîche and maple syrup, or make the coconut whipped cream.

To serve, top the warm crumble with maple crème fraîche or coconut whipped cream.

GF* For gluten-free, use gluten-free oats.

V* For vegan, top with coconut whipped cream.

FOR THE CRUMBLE

- 1½ pounds tart apples (about 4 to 5 large Granny Smith, Jonathan, or Jonagold)
- 2 teaspoons lemon zest
- ⅓ cup light brown sugar
- 1 teaspoon cinnamon
- ½ teaspoon ground cardamom
- ¾ cup dried tart cherries (no sugar added)
- 2 tablespoons cornstarch
- 1 cup oat flour or 1 cup finely ground rolled oats
- 1¼ cups rolled oats
- ¼ teaspoon kosher salt
- ⅓ cup chopped pecans
- 5 tablespoons coconut oil, at room temperature
- 6 tablespoons pure maple syrup

FOR THE TOPPING

- ½ cup crème fraîche (page 139) or coconut whipped cream (page 236)
- 1 tablespoon pure maple syrup

Vanilla-Orange Strawberry Shortcakes

I'll never forget my first bite of a local Indiana strawberry. The tiny red nuggets nestled together in a turquoise cardboard carton were picture-perfect—and the taste was intensely sweet, juicy ecstasy. Our go-to complement to summer berries is a splash of balsamic, fresh garden mint, and these shortcakes—orange-scented and lightly crunchy from glittery turbinado sugar. This dessert is well loved by our friends and family, and we're happy to give away our secrets.

Serves **8**

FOR THE SHORTCAKES

- 1 cup all-purpose flour
- ¼ cup whole wheat flour
- 2 teaspoons baking powder
- ⅓ cup turbinado raw cane sugar, plus more for dusting
- ½ teaspoon kosher salt
- ¼ cup cold unsalted butter
- Zest of ½ orange
- 1 cup plain Greek yogurt
- 2 teaspoons vanilla extract

FOR SERVING

- 1 pound ripe strawberries
- 2 tablespoons pure maple syrup
- 2 teaspoons balsamic vinegar
- Sweetened Whipped Cream (page 236)
- 10 fresh mint leaves

Preheat the oven to 400°F.

Make the shortcakes: In a medium bowl, combine the all-purpose flour, whole wheat flour, baking powder, sugar, and kosher salt. Slice the butter into thin pieces and cut it into the flour mixture using a pastry cutter or fork until it is well integrated and crumbly. Wash and dry the orange, then add the orange zest to the dough. Stir in the Greek yogurt and vanilla extract until a sticky dough forms and the flour is integrated.

Grease a muffin tin and place an even amount of the dough into 8 muffin cups. Sprinkle the tops of the cakes with extra turbinado sugar. Bake for 15 to 20 minutes until the tops are lightly browned. Remove to a wire rack to cool for 15 minutes.

Prepare the toppings: Hull and slice the strawberries. In a medium bowl, combine the strawberries with the maple syrup and balsamic vinegar and let stand at room temperature until serving, stirring occasionally.

Make the whipped cream. Thinly slice the mint.

To serve, slice each shortcake in half. Add the strawberries, dollop with whipped cream, sprinkle with fresh mint, and top with the remaining half of the cake.

Notes
Storage: The cakes can be frozen for up to 1 month. Before serving, thaw to room temperature, then warm for a few minutes in a 375°F oven.

Chocolate Mousse

with Toasted Meringue

There's nothing Alex loves more than an excuse to play with fire. Summer and fall evenings are ripe for bonfires in our fire pit—including s'mores. Here's a deconstructed, elevated take on that classic American dessert. Instead of graham crackers, there's an almond-cinnamon crunch, the chocolate layer is a chocolate mousse, and the marshmallow is a homemade meringue. It hits all the right notes for a dessert: rich, not too heavy, and visually stunning. It's also an opportune excuse for using a kitchen torch, which blackens the contours of the meringue to look like a fire-toasted marshmallow.

GF | *Serves 6*

1 cup semisweet chocolate chips, divided

1 cup heavy whipping cream

½ cup roasted salted almonds

½ teaspoon cinnamon

2 egg whites

⅛ teaspoon cream of tartar

¼ cup granulated sugar

Scant ⅛ teaspoon nutmeg

Make the chocolate mousse: Place ¾ cup chocolate chips in a glass measuring cup. Fill a large skillet halfway with water and heat to a low simmer. Once the water is simmering, turn off the heat and place the measuring cup in the water, then stir until the chocolate is just melted. Remove from the heat.

In a stand mixer with the whisk attachment (or with a hand mixer), beat the whipping cream on high for about 1 minute, until soft peaks form. Pour in the melted chocolate and continue beating for several seconds until pillowy and fully combined. Divide the mousse into 6 small glasses, bowls, or canning jars* and refrigerate for about 1 hour. Wash out the bowl of the stand mixer.

Make the almond layer: Finely chop the almonds. In a small bowl, stir them together with the cinnamon. Set aside.

Make the meringue: As close as possible to serving time, return the skillet of water to just barely a simmer. Separate the egg whites into a small bowl. In the bowl from the stand mixer (or a heatproof bowl if using a hand mixer), place the egg whites, cream of tartar, sugar, and nutmeg. Hold the bowl just touching the warm water and stir with a wooden spoon until the sugar is dissolved and the mixture is fully combined and no longer gritty, about 2 minutes. (Be careful not to overheat as the eggs could start to cook.) Move the mixing bowl to the stand mixer and attach the whisk attachment. Beat the mixture on high for about 5 minutes, until it is bright white and glossy with stiff peaks.

Assemble the parfaits: Top each glass of chocolate mousse with a handful of the almond mixture, then add the remaining ¼ cup chocolate chips divided between the glasses. Use a small spatula to top each jar with meringue and form it into peaks. Use a kitchen torch to brown the outside of each meringue for a few seconds, or toast the parfaits under a broiler for 2 minutes.* Serve immediately.

Notes

*If using a broiler, make sure the glass size allows for plenty of headroom in the oven.

Make ahead: Assemble the mousse and store refrigerated, then assemble the almonds and store in a sealed container at room temperature. As close as possible prior to serving, make the meringue and assemble the parfaits. Avoid refrigerating the meringue, as it becomes tough when chilled.

Creamy Chai Chocolate Chunk Ice Cream

This recipe reveals all our secrets for the creamiest vegan ice cream. We use full-fat coconut milk, cornstarch to thicken, and coconut oil for a bit of richness. The final trick is blending the mixture before freezing it, which helps to prevent ice crystals. The resulting ice cream is supremely creamy and stays scoopable even after freezing overnight. Our unique method for adding chocolate chunks is based on one of our favorite brands of ice cream, Graeter's. The irregular fudgy bits are suspended in the ice cream, perfect for hunting and digging out the biggest ones.

GF | **V*** | *Makes* **1 QUART**

- 2 15-ounce cans full-fat coconut milk
- 2 tablespoons cornstarch
- ½ cup agave syrup
- 2 tablespoons coconut oil
- ¼ teaspoon ground cinnamon
- ¼ teaspoon dried ground ginger
- ¼ teaspoon ground cloves
- ¼ teaspoon ground cardamom
  Pinch kosher salt
- 2 teaspoons vanilla extract
- 3 ounces high-quality dark chocolate*

Freeze the ice cream maker base overnight.

Make the ice cream: In a small bowl, mix ½ cup of the coconut milk with the cornstarch and set it aside. Add the remainder of the coconut milk to a medium saucepan. Warm the coconut milk over medium-low heat for a few minutes, whisking to incorporate the solids. Add the agave syrup, coconut oil, cinnamon, ginger, cloves, cardamom, and kosher salt, then whisk in the cornstarch mixture. Simmer gently until the mixture is thickened and coats the back of a spoon, about 5 to 6 minutes.

Remove from the heat and stir in the vanilla extract. Use an immersion blender or regular blender to blend the mixture for 1 minute.

Pour the mixture into a 1-gallon sealable plastic bag. Line a large bowl with a layer of ice cubes and place the bag with the ice cream on top. Top with another layer of ice cubes and allow to sit for 30 minutes until the mixture is cool. (Alternatively, refrigerate 4 hours or overnight.)

Make the chocolate chunks: Place the chocolate in a glass measuring cup with 2 teaspoons water. Fill a large skillet halfway with water and bring to a simmer; once the water is simmering, turn off the heat and place the measuring cup in the water, then stir until the chocolate is fully melted.

Line a baking sheet with parchment paper or a silicone mat. Spread the chocolate in a thin layer onto the parchment paper and freeze for 10 minutes. Quickly break the chocolate into large chunks with your fingers or a knife, and then return them to the freezer until ready to churn.

Churn the ice cream: Churn the ice cream in an ice cream maker until it thickens to the consistency of soft serve. Once the ice cream is fully frozen and fluffy, add the chocolate chunks, if using, and churn until fully incorporated.

Freeze the ice cream (optional): Eat immediately for a soft-serve consistency, or freeze for 3 hours for a hard ice cream texture. Press a piece of parchment or waxed paper into a sealable container and scrape the ice cream into the container. Freeze until hard, about 3 hours or overnight.

Notes

Storage: Freeze for up to 1 month.

V* For vegan, use vegan chocolate.

*Without chocolate chunks, this ice cream is ideal for topping a fruity dessert, like our apple crumble (page 251).

Metric Conversions

The recipes in this book have not been tested with metric measurements, so some variations might occur. Remember that the weight of dry ingredients varies according to the volume or density factor: 1 cup of flour weighs far less than 1 cup of sugar, and 1 tablespoon doesn't necessarily hold 3 teaspoons.

GENERAL FORMULA FOR METRIC CONVERSION

Ounces to grams .... multiply ounces by 28.35
Grams to ounces .... multiply ounces by 0.035
Pounds to grams .... multiply pounds by 453.5
Pounds to kilograms .... multiply pounds by 0.45
Cups to liters .... multiply cups by 0.24
Fahrenheit to Celsius .... subtract 32 from Fahrenheit temperature, multiply by 5, divide by 9
Celsius to Fahrenheit .... multiply Celsius temperature by 9, divide by 5, add 32

VOLUME (LIQUID) MEASUREMENTS

1 teaspoon = ⅙ fluid ounce = 5 milliliters
1 tablespoon = ½ fluid ounce = 15 milliliters
2 tablespoons = 1 fluid ounce = 30 milliliters
¼ cup = 2 fluid ounces = 60 milliliters
⅓ cup = 2 ⅔ fluid ounces = 79 milliliters
½ cup = 4 fluid ounces = 118 milliliters
1 cup or ½ pint = 8 fluid ounces = 250 milliliters
2 cups or 1 pint = 16 fluid ounces = 500 milliliters
4 cups or 1 quart = 32 fluid ounces = 1,000 milliliters
1 gallon = 4 liters

VOLUME (DRY) MEASUREMENTS

¼ teaspoon = 1 milliliter
½ teaspoon = 2 milliliters
¾ teaspoon = 4 milliliters
1 teaspoon = 5 milliliters
1 tablespoon = 15 milliliters
¼ cup = 59 milliliters
⅓ cup = 79 milliliters
½ cup = 118 milliliters
⅔ cup = 158 milliliters
¾ cup = 177 milliliters
1 cup = 225 milliliters
4 cups or 1 quart = 1 liter
½ gallon = 2 liters
1 gallon = 4 liters

WEIGHT (MASS) MEASUREMENTS

1 ounce = 30 grams
2 ounces = 55 grams
3 ounces = 85 grams
4 ounces = ¼ pound = 125 grams
8 ounces = ½ pound = 240 grams
12 ounces = ¾ pound = 375 grams
16 ounces = 1 pound = 454 grams

LINEAR MEASUREMENTS

½ in = 1 ½ cm
1 inch = 2 ½ cm
6 inches = 15 cm
8 inches = 20 cm
10 inches = 25 cm
12 inches = 30 cm
20 inches = 50 cm

OVEN TEMPERATURE EQUIVALENTS, FAHRENHEIT (F) AND CELSIUS (C)

100°F = 38°C
200°F = 95°C
250°F = 120°C
300°F = 150°C
350°F = 180°C
400°F = 205°C
450°F = 230°C

Acknowledgments

It takes an army to write a book. A heartfelt THANK YOU to:

Our agent Sarah Passick, for believing in us 1,000 percent from the start. Jessica Murnane for connecting us and being an amazing advocate, encourager, and friend.

Renee Sedliar, our dream editor and cheerleader: you helped nurture our artistic vision into being in the most positive, constructive, and encouraging way. Thank you. And the entire Da Capo team, for being collaborators to the fullest! For the gorgeous design, huge props to Alex Camlin on the cover and Tara Long on the interior.

Ashley Rodriguez, for the breathtaking watercolors and being a true supporter and friend.

Dear friends and family who lent a hand during photo shoots: Lin and Joe Gorman, Katelyn and Jared Prentice, and Dan Pino. Special thanks to the Prentices for helping brainstorm the book title.

Our recipe testers: for your enthusiasm, keen eye for detail, and willingness to try whatever we put in front of you! Your cheerleading was essential, and the connections we made will endure. You made us better recipe writers, and we are utterly grateful for your support. Thank you to:

Sarika Agarwal, Michelle Arbus, Nicholas Berkiel, Charlotte Bissutil, Hannah Botting, Chris Brown, Kelly Burson, Annie Butler, Geraldine Campbell, Christine Carlisle, Debbie Coker, Krista Convey, Rebecca Corman, Brooke Creel, Danica Crouse, Genevieve Crum, Angelina Danae, Bryan Daniel, Susan Dritt, Megan Durham, Katelyn Eling, Katie Elliott, Kay Epple, Katrin Erb, Amy Ervin, Ruth Erwin-Svoboda, Heather Evans, Ashley Farris, Dino Filippini, Elise Gahan, Jane Gardner, Mia Garuccio, David Gaudio, Igor Gejdos, Samantha Giannangeli, Stephanie Goedl, Paige Gooch, Rachel Hardacre, Shaamora Harden, Elyse Harvey, Emily Heinze, Angela Hogg, Tessa Huff, Bev and Kurt Huneck, Nadia Jagar, Steph Jenkins, Kelsey Johnson, Katie Kaminskis, Naz Karahan, Tiffany Karr, Heather Kartchner, Mia Kary, Joel Kary, Brittany Keith, Elizabeth Kellett, Maria Kennedy, Sarah Kieffer, Audra Koldyke, Kristin Kooiker, Irene Koutelieri-Aliberti, Molly Krebs, David and Kristi Kuhnau, Katie Larson, Samantha M. Leighton, Samuel Lerner, Laura Liszt,

Maeghan Livaccari, Deborah and Gary Lloyd, Carleen Logan, Katy Longworth, Vanessa MacKinnon, Shannon MacLellan, Eden Marchand, Karen Marshall, Gabrielle Martel-Rondeau, Erin Matthews, Janna Matthies, Cassandra Maynard, Kathryn McElroy, Maresa McLaren, Akua Adeneke McLeod, Julie Mennel, Abbie and Cal Meyer, Dee-Anne Miles, Emma Kruch Morris, James Moser, Rochelle Ratkaj Moser, Allison Nance, Mary Nelson, Erin and Jon Nix, Becky and Greta Novotny, Katherine Gross Nuger, Sarah O'Neall, Dina Osakue, Andy and Allison Overhiser, Joy Patel, Wilson Patton, Lia Pesce, Kiki Petersen, Rebekah Phifer, Jana du Plessis, Katelyn and Jared Prentice, Lois Pumfrey, Dolores Pyer, Colleen and Mark Richardson, Carolyn Risley, Emilie Ritchie, Kylia Robrock, Kelsie Roehl, Audrey Rood, Kate Roth, Mikaela Sanders, Katie Schmidt, Kelley Jordan Schuyler, Katharine Schwedhelm, Adity Shah, Aaryn Silva, Lauren Stark, Katie Steele, Andy Stegner, Sara Sterley, Allie Strong, Hannah Tabb, Holly Thomas, Paige Thomason, Reyna Tolentino, Laura Touhey, Renee Traylor, Mary Tressider, Dalia Pedro Trujillo, Colin Ulin, Bart Upah, Katie Van Kammen, Elizabeth Vogel, Staci Walters, Emilyn Whitesell, Andy Young, Vince Yuen, Winnie Zhao, and Kirsten Zucker.

Special thanks to Rochelle Ratkaj Moser and James Moser for making almost every recipe in the book. And to Claire Waggoner, for painstakingly editing every recipe and supporting in the testing process.

Fellow bloggers, authors, and photographers who have generously given us advice, kind words, and love along the way. Notably Annie Marshall, for believing in us from the start, Sarah Copeland, Erin Loechner, Molly Yeh, Jeanine Donofrio, Jack Mathews, Kathryne Taylor, Ashley McLaughlin, Jessica Murnane, Laura Wright, Sara Forte, Melissa Coleman, Nicole Gulotta, Gena Hamshaw, Lindsay Ostrom, Erin Alderson, Ashlae Warner, Sarah Menanix, Zoe Francois, Sarah Kieffer, Shelly Westerhausen, Amelia Winslow, Robyn Downs, Amanda Paa, Lauren McDuffie, Megan Gordon, and Cheryl Sternman Rule.

All the A Couple Cooks readers, followers, and listeners over the years: your genuine support means everything to us. You are the reason we do what we do.

Our incredible families and friends: our parents, for being our greatest supporters and number one fans. Grandma and Grandpa, for loving us so well. Our siblings for cheering us on. Our nieces and nephews, for making us laugh and cooking with us. Our large and amazing extended families, Roy, Overhiser, Kuhnau, and Mellem, for supporting every step of the way. Dearest Milena and Bernd, for being constant inspiration. Kelly, for supporting us before we were Alex and Sonja. Dan, for being a fellow dreamer. Katelyn, for being our first assistant and taste tester. To our Minnesota and Indiana friends and communities: you love us so well!

To Larson, for being an incredible light and the perfect answer to thousands of prayers. You are our everything. And to Mariah, our angel.

To God, for giving us abundant life and blessings upon measure, for sustaining us through the storms.

Index

About the Authors

Sonja and Alex Overhiser are the creators of A Couple Cooks website, a collection of whole food recipes and inspiration for healthy and sustainable eating. The husband-and-wife duo cohost and produce A Couple Cooks Podcast, a show that features conversations with the freshest voices in food, including authors, farmers, and chefs. Sonja is a writer, recipe developer, and healthy and sustainable food advocate, and Alex is a food photographer and recipe developer. Their work has been featured in national online and print publications, podcasts, and television. Sonja and Alex live in Indianapolis, Indiana, with their son, Larson. They are devoted to advocating for good, sustainable food and healthy cooking in Indianapolis, America, and beyond.